Outside of me Right

FRANKIE DOLAN

WITH DAN DOONER

HERO BOOKS

The St. James Mineola
190 2nd St., Mineola, NY
www.thestjamesmineola.com

Outside of the Right

FRANKIE DOLAN

WITH DAN DOONER

The St. James Mineola
190 2nd St., Mineola, NY
www.thestjamesmineola.com

HERO BOOKS

PUBLISHED BY HERO BOOKS
1 WOODVILLE GREEN
LUCAN
CO. DUBLIN
IRELAND

Hero Books is an imprint of Umbrella Publishing
First Published 2021
Copyright © Frankie Dolan and Dan Dooner 2021
All rights reserved

A CIP record for this book is available from the British Library

ISBN 9781910827291

Cover design and formatting: jessica@viitaladesign.com
Ebook formatting: www.ebooklaunch.com
Photographs: The Dolan family collection and Sportsfile

Dedication

To My Parents
Frank and Rosaleen

Contents

Acknowledgements

WITHOUT THE SUPPORT of my parents Frank and Rosaleen I would have had no chance of having the career I had in soccer and Gaelic football. They drove me all over the country. Their support was there for me every single day. And I have to thank them, first and foremost, for helping me to become the man I am today.

There were other people, too, of course.

I must thank all of the coaches I trained with in both sports, from underage, through my teens and into adulthood. Those who I got on well with, and also those I found 'difficult'. I want to thank each and every one of you – I learned something from everyone.

To all my teammates, from club and county, I was lucky to share a dressing-room with you all and make so many friends for life.

To the boys who climbed the steps of the Hogan Stand with me in 2013, and your partners, and St Brigid's team management and club officials, thank you for making my dreams come true.

CAROLINE, RYEN AND JACK!

Words cannot describe what you mean to me.

Your patience for putting up with all of the constant talk about football and, for you Caroline, without your loving and constant support over the years – and allowing me all of the time I am away from home on foobtall 'duty' – none of my story would be in a book today.

Also, without the support of Caroline's mother and father Aideen and Padraig, our lives would have been much harder. They have given of their time unreservedly over the last few years minding our lads, again allowing me the opportunity to continue coaching and managing, and being involved with teams. Padraig was also on my shoulder for a period when I managed St Brigid's and he acted as our kit man.

I feel the luckiest man in the world to have Ryen and Jack, and to have the honour of training you in the Roscommon Gaels Academy. I might annoy you both daily about soccer and GAA, but you know I wish for you to follow your dreams, whatever they are, wherever they make take you – and never forget, your Mammy and Daddy will always do everything we can to help you fulfil those same dreams.

TO MY GREAT friend and fellow Rossie Kieran Keaveney and his wife Tracey, who are now living in New York, thank you for being such a generous sponsor (www.thestjamesmineola.com) of my memoir – I look forward to meeting up soon in your new restaurant and bar in New York City, The St James Gate, and sharing a few old stories over a couple of cold beers. I am so proud to have such brilliant friends, and I wish you both all the success in the world with your new venture.

TO ALL MY friends, family members, and those of you who have helped me in any small way down through the years – thank you from the bottom of my heart.

To my club St Brigid's where I spent over 20 years playing senior football, making friends for life, and falling out with the occasional person also. Thank you for providing me and my teammates with some of the best coaches and facilities anyone could wish for, and for your support and devotion to our cause.

To Ballymahon GAA, who I was lucky and privileged to play with for two years, thank you for taking me under your wing, and for allowing me to help make history for the club. And thank you to my teammates for making me feel so welcome.

To Roscommon GAA, for giving me the chance to represent my county with such pride. Thank you always.

TO DAN DOONER, my 'ghost writer', for your massive amount of work in piecing my story together in this memoir. We really got to know one another over the last year, mostly over Zoom, regrettably, but I always enjoyed the banter and the craic, and reminiscing on the great and not so great days.

At times, Dan, you were more of a counsellor than a journalist, and I can safely say we will be friends for life after this.

And to Anna, Dan's fiancée, thank you for being so understanding with both of us over the last 12 months or so. I wish you both all the health and happiness for the future.

Finally, to Liam Hayes and Hero Books, I have to say a massive thank you for giving me the opportunity to tell my story. It was also a privilege working with you, Liam.

I am proud of this book, though I did not build it on my own, and without my mother Rosaleen, my father Frank, my sister Kara, brothers Darren and Garvan, John 'Patsy' O'Connor, Pat Regan and Karol Mannion, I am not sure any of this would have been possible.

Frankie Dolan
April 2021

◄◄◆►►

WRITING A BOOK during a global pandemic is not an easy task but it has been an experience I'll never forget. I only hope that this is an enjoyable read for GAA supporters in Roscommon and further afield. The primrose and blue has been donned by many footballing 'Legends' and it was an honour and a privilege to document the life and career of one of them.

With that in mind, I want to thank Liam Hayes and everyone at Hero Books for not only trusting in me to deliver this book but also for supporting myself and Frankie Dolan throughout the process.

I have really enjoyed working with Frankie and I'm glad to say that a friendship has developed since our first chat, a friendship based on a mutual love of sport and a growing frustration with our beloved Manchester United!

Behind all the headlines is a man who wears his heart firmly on his sleeve, a trait I greatly admire. Frankie calls it as he sees it and this has led to him butting heads with managers, members of the opposition and match officials on a number of occasions in the past. Thankfully, he displayed a more patient and understanding side over the past year and was always available and ready to talk whenever I called on him! I want to thank Frankie, his wife Caroline, their two sons Ryen and Jack, and the rest of the Dolan family for giving me access to their lives, particularly during what has been a very stressful time for many.

A big thank you also to Paul and Fiona Healy and all of my colleagues at the *Roscommon People* for their support over the past year and in years previous. I'm lucky to enjoy the work I do and a big part of that is down to the team I work with.

I want to also acknowledge the love and support of both my own family and the Ryan family, especially my mother, the real Saint Brigid! It has been a difficult year for all of us, but her support remains unwavering. Thank you for everything you do!

Last but certainly not least, a very special thank you to my wife-to-be and proud Rossie Anna Ryan. God knows it's not easy living with me at the best of times, so thank you for your love and support, and above all your patience, throughout this process.

Dan Dooner
April 2021

PROLOGUE

Prologue

A cold Tuesday night in Kiltoom…

I WAS SITTING with the club solicitor Jimmy Mannion in his car outside the St Brigid's clubhouse. We were getting ready to head off to the county board offices in Roscommon town.

Jimmy was in the middle of briefing me on what lay ahead.

'Now gossun, you're not to tell the whole truth in there. Just stick to the script and leave most of the talking to me,' he said as he smacked my chest to reinforce every word.

'Okay Jimmy, I'll just follow your lead. Whatever you say.'

We pulled up outside the county board offices, which were located just behind Rockfords Nightclub in those days – another place I had become familiar with over the years. Memories of sitting outside the principal's office in Ballybay and Athlone came flooding back and the butterflies started to flutter in the pit of my stomach.

'Remember Frankie… stick to the story!'

THE OLD ROSCOMMON county board offices were hardly modern, and they certainly weren't inviting on nights like that.

The disciplinary committees themselves were never the most welcoming either and they seemed to get a kick out of keeping you waiting. Twenty minutes passed and there was no sign of anyone.

'They're probably in there, drinking their tea and talking shite,' I muttered to Jimmy.

'They probably are but maybe don't mention that when you're in there,' he said, not looking up from his notes.

Suddenly, the door swung open and we were summoned into the room. Sitting in front of us was the three-man appeals committee.

'Good evening lads,' Jimmy said, and they grunted something in return.

THOSE PANELS WERE always the same and you got to know all the lads from different clubs around Roscommon.

The way they were made up was always the same too.

There was usually one fella who you think might be in your corner and another fella who you think might be on the fence and who you'd try and have the craic with. Get two out of three on your side and that would do.

But then there was usually an auld fella who didn't say much. He was old school and believed the referee's report was Gospel, and that the sun shone out of his arse. The auld lad is only there for the free tea and biscuits, the bit of gossip... and to f**k you and your club up any way he can.

IT DIDN'T TAKE ME too long though to learn that things usually weren't as they seemed.

The fella I had the craic with was the one that was out to get me... and the one who was supposed to be on the fence was actually fairly sound.

The committees are supposed to be democratic though and so that means the older fella usually had the deciding vote.

That's when I knew I was in trouble!

A traditional Roscommon GAA man, he had little time for the Dolans or the St Brigid's' of this world, I felt.

EVERY TIME I walked into the county board offices for those hearings it felt like I was going there with cap in hand, begging to be allowed to continue playing football.

Nine times out of 10 I was wasting my time with those dinosaurs, unless there was clear video evidence that contradicted the referee's report.

Most of the time I would end up making my way back to Kiltoom, my tail between my legs. The dreaded appeals process began as soon as the club secretary received an email about a sending off a few days after a game. You had a couple of days to decide if you wanted to appeal and that's when the questions began to churn around in my head.

Is it worth it? Have they got me by the balls? Do I really want the hassle?

Springtime 2006

MOST OF THE TIME it's far easier to just take your medicine and sit it out for a while. Like the time I was sent off in the very first minute of a meaningless league match against Boyle in Kiltoom.

I had been at a stag party the night before and had absolutely zero interest in anything other than a few pints to cure my hangover the next day. I had even been honest with the team management in the run-up to the game. I told them about the stag and my feelings about playing the match with a fuzzy head.

There was no day off.

Just be there, they told me.

'That's fine lads.'

Out on the beer I went.

JIMMY REILLY WAS the referee that day. Jimmy's a man I've always had time for and one who doesn't suffer any bullshit. You can have the craic with Jimmy and chat away to him, as long as you know that once a decision is made then that is it.

Jimmy threw the ball in to start the match and Mark O'Carroll rose highest and won possession, but he overcooked his kick pass and it flew straight over my head and into the hands of the Boyle full-back. This fella is hopping the ball and running forward in my direction. I can still see him coming. He has a bit of a ponytail – not really my cup of tea, but whatever. I have my mind made up.

BANG!

I flip him and his ponytail upside down with a clothesline. Thirty seconds gone and players from both sides are standing there in silence. Jimmy, the referee, is running towards me, but I already know what's coming... I'm walking to the sideline before he takes out his red card.

I wasn't proud of the 'tackle', but I was secretly relieved I wouldn't have to play on. I didn't want to be there, and I had made that clear. It's rare that I don't want to be involved in a game of football, so I thought they'd understand and let me off for once. No chance.

I could have no complaints about any ban following that incident and deep down I knew it would only add to my poor reputation among the Roscommon GAA authorities.

Good job that wasn't something I had ever lost sleep over anyway. I even invited Jimmy to our wedding!

November 2006

WHILE THAT INCIDENT stands out as one for which I deserved my punishment, there were other occasions when I felt I had been hard done by.

Like when I had a run-in with one of the Corofin mentors during our 2006 Connacht final at Dr Hyde Park.

The game was only 34 minutes old, and David O'Connor, who's better known by his nickname 'Jimmy Nail', had got involved with the Corofin star Gary Sice off the ball.

Jimmy Nail ended up giving Sice a bit of a slap and the Galway man went down.

Vincent Neary from Mayo was the referee that day and he'd already booked Jimmy Nail and sent off one of their lads after just three minutes. I tried to pick Sice off the ground before Neary took it upon himself to even up the numbers.

Two of the Corofin lads Kieran McGrath and Kieran Fitzgerald then started having a go at me. It was nothing serious, just handbags really.

While we were grappling, this older fella appeared from nowhere in between them. There was no mentor bib, so I just assumed he was a supporter.

I swung for him and ended up clocking him in the jaw. The two Kierans definitely weren't happy now.

It turned out it was Gary Sice's father Jimmy who was also a selector with Corofin.

Honestly, I had no idea who he was at the time. I just saw this fella dressed in dark clothing running towards me. The Corofin supporters said he was only coming on to tend to his son.

Neary didn't see the incident and neither did any of his officials. I was off the hook that day and could play on. However, the incident was caught on video and in a couple of photographs, and it wasn't long before I was summoned to a meeting with the Connacht Games Administration Committee.

THE INITIAL BAN of six months was severe and would have seen me missing out on the All-Ireland semi-final the following spring against Crossmaglen. Thankfully, it was reduced to three months on appeal, which I still thought was harsh for defending myself against three hardy Corofin men!

Eleven years later, our paths crossed in the Connacht final once again, in Tuam, when I was managing St Brigid's. Jimmy was still part of the Corofin backroom by this stage and it was the first time I had seen him since that day at the Hyde. We spoke, I apologised for lashing out, and I'm glad to say we could laugh about it in the end.

November 2013

THE MOST INFAMOUS disciplinary incident I was involved in went all the way to the Dispute Resolutions Authority at Croke Park.

It came following an incident after the full-time whistle of our Connacht final defeat to Castlebar Mitchels at Dr Hyde Park in 2013. We were the defending All-Ireland and Connacht champions that year and we fancied our chances against the Mayo side.

You can call it sour grapes if you want, but we still believe Mitchels got too many decisions that day from Sligo referee Marty Duffy and his officials.

We were leading by a point in second-half injury-time when one of the Mitchels' backs kicked the ball over the sideline and gave us a lineball at their end of the pitch.

Great... an opportunity to keep the ball inside their half and run down the clock. Duffy had other ideas, however, and overruled his linesman, giving Mitchels possession and just enough time for one last attack.

It all went downhill from there.

They booted the ball into our half and worked it to within shooting distance, forcing Ian Kilbride to commit a foul right in front of the posts. It was an innocuous tackle, but Duffy adjudged it to be a red card offence and sent Killer to the line.

Talk about rubbing salt into an open wound.

Mitchels went on to win it in extra-time but not before Duffy sent Darragh Donnelly and Richie Blaine off too. Our Connacht title was gone and our dream of back-to-back All-Irelands was over. To say we felt aggrieved would have been a massive understatement. We were beside ourselves.

My first thought was to locate my brother Garvan, who was never a man to take a defeat like that without having something to say.

I could see Garvan on the other side of the pitch, making a beeline for Duffy. *Marty could be in bother here*, I thought.

I ran towards Garv and with help from one of our supporters, just about managed to drag him away and get him sitting down in the dugouts.

A lucky escape.

AFTER A FEW MINUTES it felt like the storm had passed. Garvan was calm by then and the game was over so there was nothing we could do anyway.

At that moment, a group of officials walked past us. I had my back to them as I continued to talk to Garvan.

Someone muttered, 'Take your beating!'

I backed into them before swinging around in a rage.

The linesman whose decision had been overturned by Duffy at the end of normal time was standing there.

I lost it a little bit and got right in his face.

There were plenty of harsh words exchanged and I had to be pulled away, but I can say, hand on heart, that there was little or no physical contact whatsoever. And I stand by that to this day.

I was still licking my wounds the following week when the club secretary called to tell me that there had been an email, and the news wasn't good.

'A 48-week ban for striking an official'. It was pure bullshit.

There were also bans for Garv and Killer. Sixty-four weeks in total for the three of us. Madness.

The club agreed straight away that we should appeal the suspensions, so the 'terrible three' were dispatched to Bekan, Ballyhaunis for a meeting with the wise men of the Connacht Disciplinary Committee.

We were lucky at the club that we had the likes of the late Jimmy Mannion to fight our corner. Jimmy was a gentleman and was so reassuring during those hearings.

This time around, however, our representative would be Senan and Ian's father Seán and he looked the part with a briefcase full of papers. I'm still not sure if those papers had anything to do with our appeals, but they looked good anyway!

WE ARRIVED AT the room up in Bekan and members of the committee were lounging around watching a Man United match. One of them nearly sent the tea and biscuits flying as he scrambled to turn off the TV.

Garvan was his usual diplomatic self.

'Ah sure leave it on!' he says, 'It can't be as bad as some of the other shite you have to deal with.'

Our former manager Kevin McStay was there as part of our defence that day.

'I was at the game and I saw what happened. Frankie did not hit any official,' said the former Mayo All Star and our star witness.

If that doesn't sway them, I thought.

Seán Kilbride is another authoritative figure, and he did his best to paint us as three choir boys from Kiltoom.

It was all a waste of time. The jury was always going to be reluctant to overrule Marty and his officials and, in the end, they refused to budge.

We were due to head out to Berlin that week for a well-earned break and so there was only one thing for it as we made our way home to Kiltoom that evening… a few pints in a pub in Ballinlough.

Soon we were laughing about the whole Bekan episode and looking forward to our trip to Germany. Further appeals could wait until we got back.

EAMON O'ROURKE WAS a long-time supporter of the club and a great friend and father figure to me down through the years. He sponsored our little trip to Europe that year, which was greatly appreciated by a group of lads who had been on the road for the previous three years together.

The party started the moment we left Kiltoom and continued for four days in Berlin. It was just what we all needed after losing our Connacht crown in such a frustrating way.

We were still bitterly disappointed of course and there was talk of lads stepping away. It was something that crossed my own mind after the Castlebar game too. I felt the body was more or less done, and at the age of 36, a 48-week ban could well have forced my hand. It would be a sad way to end my career, but it seemed like there might be no other option.

The more I dwelled on it in Berlin though, the more I realised I just wasn't ready to hang up the boots. By the time I got back to Roscommon, I had my mind made up. With nothing to lose, it was decided I would appeal the ban all the way to the DRA at Croke Park.

It turned out to be a surreal experience.

January 2014

I REMEMBER WE were brought into one of those suites at premium level before the hearing got underway and there, spread out on tables, was every kind of sandwich you could think of as well as tea, coffee, cappuccinos, and biscuits. Had I known what kind of hospitality was on offer, I would have appealed every one of my suspensions to the lads on the DRA!

The appeals panel was made up of representatives from Ulster, Munster, Leinster and Connacht and there were two other officials from our province there too. Jimmy Mannion was drafted in for the special occasion. It was a day for the big hitters and Jimmy was very convincing as he fought our case.

We were helped by the fact that one of the Connacht officials clearly didn't have his homework done properly and really struggled with one of the questions Jimmy put to him about the referee's report. Looking around the room, I could see the other officials looking at each other and almost rolling their eyes. It felt like a slight breakthrough. Maybe I'd get to postpone the retirement after all!

LATER THAT NIGHT, as we made our way home to Roscommon after the hearing, Jimmy got word that the suspension had been halved. It was now just six months and had started from the end of the Connacht final, which meant I wouldn't miss much in the early months of 2014. I could now enjoy a break from the league games and recharge the batteries ahead of a return to training in May for the championship.

The idea of walking away from playing scared me and I still believed I had something to offer the team. I drove back to Roscommon that night both reprieved and relieved.

July 2020

INCIDENTS ALWAYS GROW legs, especially in a small county like Roscommon. Some people can become caricatures of themselves and their reputation suffers badly as a result. There have been times when this has happened to me and no matter what I said or how hard I tried, some people had me pegged as some sort of thug on the pitch and an ill-disciplined party boy off it.

I believe the narrative that I was an egomaniac who fell out with managers, officials and other authority figures as soon as things didn't go my way was also false.

People saw me on their television screens or read about me in some newspaper article, and straight away they thought they had me sussed out. They didn't always appreciate the fact that behind a heated incident or a red card, or even some drunken game of pool in Derry, there was just a normal guy with the same problems as everyone else.

OF COURSE, THERE were plenty of occasions during my Roscommon career when the term 'discipline problem' was used as a reason for why I had fallen out of favour with some managers. That was a cop out.

Players with genuine discipline problems do not perform at the highest level for 20 years. They don't show up for training every week or help drive their teammates on to All-Ireland glory. They don't insist on attending club training while still in the thick of the county's championship campaign either.

Only players who genuinely love the game, their club and their county would put themselves through all of that.

That's why I did it, and the pleasure and privilege was all mine.

PART ONE

Who I Am

« CHAPTER 1 »

THE ALARM CLOCK goes off at half six every morning and I'm up out of bed, looking for the uniform, before grabbing a quick breakfast and heading out the door for work.

My workday starts at half past seven at the An Post mail centre in Roscommon town, where I load up the post for my daily run and jump in the van. There's nobody to annoy me in that van, it's just me and the radio. By half past eight I'm singing along on the road to Rahara and St John's, just a former St Brigid's footballer delivering more good and bad news in St Dominic's territory!

I really enjoy the work. There are plenty of cold and wet days, but I'd take bad weather over sitting in some air-conditioned office, confined to a desk, any day of the week. I'm probably too wild to be locked up in one building all day anyway. I love the freedom of being out on the road. Driving up and down country lanes, and meeting all sorts of characters along the way.

There have been many changes in the towns and villages since I started with An Post in 2004. During that time, local pubs and businesses as well as most services have closed down. Local Garda stations have shut and even the post office in Knockcroghery has come under threat from Government cutbacks. The whole social fabric of rural Roscommon has changed too, as people have fewer and fewer places to meet and chat.

Of course, thanks to Covid-19, there have also been huge changes in the past year too. It's amazing when you consider what we used to take for granted. I meet people every day who long for the days when they could simply call into a neighbour or spend some time chatting as they collected their pension or posted a letter.

The pandemic has really affected them and so now they stop me and anyone else who happens to come their way for a quick chat.

'What do ya think of that Trump fella?'

'That's a fine young Brigid's team.'

'They've still got a lot to prove… but Dominic's are going well.'

'United were brutal last night!'

They will chat about anything and everything just to have that connection with someone. The lockdowns have made me more conscious of the people I meet along the route who may go from one end of the week to the other without any meaningful social interaction. It is not a healthy position to be in at any age, but especially in later years. Rural isolation is real, and I see the effects of it every day. The Covid-19 pandemic has only brought it to the fore.

THERE ARE A lot of people who either don't have family or have been prevented from seeing them. The loneliness some people must feel is unimaginable.

As the local postman, that puts me in a unique and very privileged position. I believe I have a responsibility as a member of An Post to reach out and make that connection with people, even if it means just checking in with elderly residents or those living alone. I'm always happy to be able to offer help to the community and there's always a great feeling of satisfaction and a bit of pride when I get back to the mail centre at the end of my shift.

Being a former Roscommon footballer helps to spark those connections with people too. It's a great icebreaker for some people. They'll recognise me from the telly or from being at matches, and it'll trigger a memory.

Some memories are better than others.

'That was some score that day in Portlaoise!'

'What did you say to your man that day? He was like a bull!'

'What's this fascination with lads stripping off together anyway?'

There's a fair bit of slagging at times but people are welcoming and generous once they get to know you. Sometimes they're too generous, and if I accepted every offer of a cup of tea that came my way, it would take me the week to complete my round!

IT IS MY pleasure to be able to keep those people company if only for a short while each day, and to deliver any messages or prescriptions they might need. I feel as though I am making a slight difference.

My day job has also brought home to me the importance of Roscommon supporters meeting those who have been lucky enough to have worn the primrose and blue. The way the game has gone over the last few years means that this doesn't happen naturally anymore. It's nobody's fault. It was different during my time because we would usually arrive in for a pint after the game. It is impossible for players to do that now with the levels of fitness needed to compete at the top level.

But from what I've seen over the last few years, the Roscommon players are excellent at making themselves available for supporters in other ways. I am glad though that there weren't as many 'selfie' requests back in my day! Working in the community is not just a great way of meeting people and chatting about football, it also allows supporters to get to know the real me.

To some, I'm still the controversial former Roscommon footballer Frankie Dolan. A fella who walked away from county panels or who fell out with every manager who had the cheek to drop him. Some opinions of me are even based on something that may have been heard in the pub one night.

Some people really do believe everything they see on the television or read on social media. Gossip is quick to spread in a county like Roscommon, and people can quickly form the wrong impression.

I sometimes compare it to being a wrestler in the World Wrestling Federation or a boxer trying to hype up a fight. There's the on-field persona and the actual person away from the sport. There are times when you are playing a character on the pitch so you can get the best out of yourself and your teammates, but that doesn't mean it's who you are the other six days of the week.

A lot of incidents that get highlighted on TV are part and parcel of the game. The adrenaline is pumping through your veins and it can bring out the best or the worst in you. From my own point of view, it didn't help that I hated losing and that I would seek to gain whatever advantage I could for both myself and my team.

I never did anything in a malicious way, I was just trying to level the playing field when we came up against sides who were that little bit cuter than we are. Back then, from 2001 to '05 and beyond, all the top county sides were at it. The 'dark arts' as it became known. There were times when I felt Roscommon players were a bit naïve when it came to this side of the game.

Maybe that's why I stood out like a sore thumb in the county.

Those who know me best would tell you that the off-field persona is quite different to that 'lunatic' who sometimes appeared on your TV screen. I'd be the very first to admit that I can be pig-headed – it's a Dolan family trait! If I don't agree with something or if I don't think things are being done in the right way, then I'll have no problem in saying so.

My sister Kara compares me to Roy Keane. And I could be wrong, but I don't think it's because of my ability on the soccer pitch.

There were plenty of days when I would be involved in a row during a game or some heated argument afterwards before landing back in the clubhouse for a pint. I'd be chatting away to people and having the craic while watching whatever match was on TV. Just one of the lads.

Up at the bar, I'd often overhear people talking about me...

'Jaysus, Dolan's actually alright!'

'Maybe he's calmed down.'

It could be a bit embarrassing really, wondering if that was what most people were saying about me. Part of me wanted to assure them I wasn't the big bad wolf they thought I was or that the Frankie they read about or saw on TV wasn't the real me. So, who am I then?

I'M JUST A normal fella who gets up every morning and goes to work to provide for my wife Caroline and our two sons. I wear my heart on my sleeve and I'm at my happiest chatting to people and having the craic.

In the evenings and at weekends, I am still involved in Gaelic football, both as a coach and manager, and as someone who helps with the Roscommon Gaels nursery where my two boys Ryen and Jack play.

It drives Caroline mad, but I rarely turn down a request to help with a training session or to drop in and talk to a group of players, whether it's underage ladies' football or a senior men's team. Football's *football* and I'm thankful that I still love the game and that I'm able to give something back to it.

The lights have long faded on my own playing career, and while coaching might not have the same buzz as parading around Croke Park for an All-Ireland club final or running out in front of 30,000 people at Dr Hyde Park for a big championship match, Gaelic football is something I simply could not live without.

My reputation with Roscommon might suggest that I'm an egomaniac or some sort of maverick, but I have never asked or wanted to be treated any differently to anyone else. My biggest problem was with the direction in which county football was headed. It pains me to see the way it has gone. Maybe it's down to social media, but some players are treated like celebrities nowadays, while the game itself has gone far too professional. I can only imagine the kind of negative coverage players would have to endure if they were caught enjoying the kind of nights out we once had.

WHILE IT HAS been tough on all of us, the one silver lining of the Covid-19 pandemic is that it has brought us all back down to earth in many ways. It has certainly shown us the importance of Gaelic games in our communities, with the club at the very heart of everything. We've seen club members reach out to elderly people and those living alone and be a force for good during some very dark times. There have always been so many examples in this country of how communities of all kinds benefit from having a GAA club as their focal point.

Whether it's a rural club like ourselves at St Brigid's or an urban club like Ballymun Kickhams, our opponents in the 2013 All-Ireland final, it's a great way of bringing people together and keeping young people on the right path.

LIKE ANY OTHER footballer or hurler, I was always proud to represent my club, my community, and my county. I may have experienced many highs and lows since breaking into the St Brigid's senior team at the age of 18 but being part of a group of like-minded people was something which always gave me peace of mind and a purpose. When I felt as though I was heading in the wrong direction or when things were getting hard at home, the glow of the floodlights in Kiltoom would guide me back to where I felt most at ease.

Football remains my biggest passion, but it's only ever been a part of who I really am.

« CHAPTER 2 »

THE WAY MY mother tells it, herself and the father were driving an old banger of a car around the time she was expecting me.

They were living and working in Athlone at the time, which in those days was still a bit of a drive to the maternity ward in Portiuncula Hospital in Ballinalsoe. When she started experiencing contractions, my father helped her out to the car and they tore off towards Ballinasloe.

It wasn't long, however, before the car started to splutter, and cut out. You can imagine my mother's panic at that time, but also my father's... when the blue lights appeared in his rear-view mirror. Luckily for Frank Snr, there aren't too many officers of the law who'd chance challenging Rosaleen Haugh at the best of times, never mind when she was about to go into labour.

A Garda escort later, and I was ready to come into the world kicking and screaming at Portiuncula on Saturday, July 22, 1978, the first child born to Frank and Rosaleen Dolan. Not even out of the womb, and already attracting the attention of the authorities!

If the fortunes of Roscommon football were anything to go by, I had picked the perfect moment to make my grand entrance. One of the great Roscommon teams had beaten Galway in the Connacht final just a couple of weeks before, while the under-21s would soon become All-Ireland champions. It was a glorious summer to be a Rossie.

The three of us began our life together in Athlone, before my sister Kara and brothers Garvan and Darren joined us over the course of the next 12 years. During this time, we moved from the garrison town to rural south Roscommon, where our parents had built our new home.

Our family were certainly no strangers to this part of the world. We would often hear tales of how our grandfather, Frank or 'The Culch' as he was known, would spend his days cycling out towards Lough Funshinagh between Rahara and Kiltoom to hunt ducks and geese. It was a round trip of about 30 miles and he would hang whatever he managed to shoot on the crossbar of his High Nelly and then make his way back to Athlone as it started to get dark. This was when he wasn't busy with his day job with the ESB, of course.

There was one goose which managed to avoid the handlebars of Frank's bicycle, however. The Culch had managed to clip this one's wing rather than killing it during one of his shooting sessions. He took pity on it and brought it home as a pet. He had that goose for a few weeks, too. He used to tie it up out near the lake and use it as a way of luring other geese into his sights.

The goose had only begun to enjoy its new life with Frank until one day it was shot in a case of mistaken identity. Another fella had spotted it from behind a bush, but didn't realise it was now domesticated. He took aim and fired, finishing the job Frank had started a few weeks before. The Culch wasn't too pleased, and it's said that some stern words were exchanged.

Frank was a well-known character around Athlone but enjoyed the peace and quiet out in the Roscommon countryside near the 'disappearing lake', Lough Funshinagh.

It's a nice coincidence that my route with An Post takes me out there each morning, but I don't know what The Culch would make of the lake now as it continues to flood farms and homes, and shows no signs of disappearing.

The Dolan family began life in Court Devenish in Athlone – through the archway opposite where Burgess' clothes shop is today – when The Culch arrived from his native Galway. Born on the docks, he was an industrious man, and our father would often tell us how he used to bring home that evening's dinner from his trips to Roscommon.

The Dolans were probably the best fed family in Westmeath at the time, living on Frank Snr's supplies of duck, pheasant, goose, rabbit, salmon, and trout.

Along with being a successful hunter and fisherman, our grandfather was also a keen sportsman. He was a rower on the River Corrib in Galway and on the Shannon in Athlone. He was also a founding member of the Athlone Anglers Association and most of his children would grow up with a keen love of sport.

As well as my father Frank, my uncles Des and Ken and my aunt Pat Fox became well-known locally through their sporting accomplishments. My father and his brothers all played for Athlone GAA and Westmeath while my aunt Pat played and coached hockey. Her sons have all achieved in sport. Morgan enjoyed some success as a pro cyclist and now has his own professional team, EvoPro Racing. Keith was a physiotherapist for Coventry City Football Club and Connacht Rugby and is currently with the Irish rugby team. Damien is a really good soccer player, while Robbie, who is currently a masseur with Connacht Rugby and getting on great there, was a talented GAA player with Garrycastle. Mark also had talent to burn on the GAA field, until he did serious damage to his knee a few years back. I really look forward to family weddings, or parties of any kind – these lads are the life and soul of every party.

There was a huge sporting tradition on that side of the family and Des's sons Dessie and Gary would go on to have successful Gaelic football careers too.

My mother's father Billy was from Eastwell, Cappataggle in Galway; her mother Mary was from Clonony More, Shannon Harbour in Birr. Billy was into the greyhounds and horses. They were married in England.

I would be in regular contact with my uncle, Tony in New York. He retired recently – he was one of those lads who drove the horses and carriages around Central Park most of his life. I loved going over to visit him.

I also loved visiting my grandparents Billy and Mary. I could end up walking one of Billy's greyhounds to Moate and back!

As a child, I knew our family was never very well-off, but my brothers, sister and I never wanted for anything. Our parents did their best to provide for us and there are plenty of happy memories of family gatherings, special events, and trips away to soccer and Gaelic football matches. We also inherited our grandfather's love for fishing and shooting. My father and uncles introduced us to these sports as soon as we were old enough to hold a shotgun.

I was just a few years old when they first brought me up the lake in a boat. It was great growing up with those hobbies and I used to spend weeks looking forward to the fishing and shooting competitions my father had entered me in. It wasn't long before Garvan and Darren joined us on our expeditions, and you could say that all three of us have been 'hooked' ever since.

One of my most vivid memories is of my father teaching me to shoot in the back garden of our house in Barrymore. I was 11 or 12 at the time and he had a side-by-side shotgun. I was mad to have a go at it, but back then there was a fierce kick-back from those guns, and my mother wasn't too keen on the idea of arming me!

The father agreed to let me have a go anyway and I still remember my nerves as he threw an empty orange can into the air and I steadied the gun and took aim.

BANG! I hit the target with my first shot and bits of aluminium flew all over the garden. From my father's point of view, it had been a successful introduction to shooting, but he had a hard time convincing the mother!

In the years that followed, the shooting and hunting would prove to be invaluable as a way of getting out in the fresh air to clear the head. Unlike football, it didn't even matter whether I hit the target or not.

The head would certainly need plenty of clearing by the time I reached adulthood. The atmosphere in the house could be a bit tough to take at times, with plenty of slamming of doors, and it began to take its toll on all of us.

While I was worried about my parents, football became another way of keeping my mind from dwelling on things. I thought about nothing else when I was out on the pitch and that helped me to get some headspace in my teens and my early twenties.

MY PARENTS SPLIT up for good when I was about 23 and by that stage it was easier to understand that it was the only real option for them. Separation still wasn't a common occurrence back then in Catholic Ireland, especially in rural Roscommon and it took me a long time to get used to the idea, but I did learn to adapt eventually.

I think it's only natural that you are drawn to your mother in these situations. That bond is almost impossible to break, particularly for Irish men. My father and I still get on well, though we probably did drift apart for a few years after he left in 2001, in the weeks following the Connacht final.

Their separation left a lasting effect.

MY FATHER HAS been a keen supporter of my football career and was always there to congratulate me or commiserate with me at the full-time whistle. I was grateful for his support and felt as though he had my back, often when I was in the wrong.

Sometimes I would even hear stories at training, or while having a pint after a match, that the auld lad was involved in a shouting match on the terraces, usually after coming to my defence. He would never have been one to back down… I suppose the acorn doesn't fall far from the tree in that regard!

While my father was a great supporter of my football, I'd be closer to my mother in many other ways. As life goes on though I probably don't get to see as much of her as I should. Work starts early in the morning and then football takes up most evenings in the week as well as large chunks of the weekend. The two boys also keep me quite busy, and so if I'm lucky, I'll get up to see her once a week.

It's the same with every family I suppose. Sometimes you go weeks without seeing each other and Covid-19 has certainly made visiting that little bit more difficult at times.

The pandemic of 2020 and '21 definitely changed the way I think about her and the rest of the family though. Life slowed down a bit during lockdown and I think it made many people realise what's important. It brought us closer as a family and we got to see more of each other. That has been one of the few positives that I have taken from a very tough period.

Despite the tension between my mother and father, it was still a good childhood and my earliest memories of life in Athlone and Kiltoom are mainly happy ones.

THE FIRST YEAR of my education took place at the Fair Green National School in Athlone, where St Mary's School is today. It was convenient for my parents because, not only was it close to our house, the two of them also worked within walking distance of the school.

Long before Skype and Zoom calls or even mobile phones, my mother was a proud employee of the Telecom Exchange in Athlone. The exchange used to be situated where Athlone Bus and Train Stations are today. My father worked just a few minutes away on Connaught Street, where he ran his own printing business.

My parents were still in the process of building what would turn out to be our family home in Kiltoom at that time. As we would learn from the reports of our grandfather's one-man shooting parties, the neighbouring county of Roscommon was 'out in the country'. It seemed like a whole other world away, at least to my young mind anyway. It should come as absolutely no surprise to those who have followed my Gaelic football career that my earliest memories of the Fair Green schoolyard in Athlone involved plenty of arguments and fist fights, with the odd game of soccer thrown in! Perhaps it was my grandfather's survival instincts rubbing off on me, but the next fight or row never seemed to be too far away. I had a habit of getting involved in the usual scrapes and scraps that many young boys experienced back then. It's fair to say that my competitive streak landed me in far more trouble than your average junior infant.

On one occasion, I was playing in one of our regular soccer matches in the yard during 'big break', when myself and my man-marker had a minor disagreement, which then escalated into open warfare. We could almost imagine the reports of the blood-soaked schoolyard in that week's *Westmeath Independent* as we stood there trading blows. In our young minds, this was box office stuff and it felt like the whole school was watching us as we tried to tear lumps out of each other.

Back in reality, we had just pushed and shoved and scratched and scraped the way young kids do when tempers have been lost and there's a fear of also losing face in front of classmates. This was no boxing masterclass, it was as disorganised as our games of football – and we were both hauled in front of the teacher to explain our involvement in the mayhem.

With my reputation and body already taking a battering in Athlone, countryside or no countryside, it came as a relief to know that my parents were building that house up in Kiltoom, and I was happy to make my escape to Ballybay National School the very next year.

My teachers at Ballybay would quickly learn that while I really enjoyed playing sports with my classmates, I wasn't destined to become one of the world's leading academic minds. My days in the classroom were spent counting down the minutes until we were let loose on the schoolyard again. That last hour until the bell sounded for us to go home seemed to drag on forever each afternoon.

Not surprisingly, I see things a bit differently now that I have my own kids. Back then I never had any real interest in my studies, and usually did just enough to get by each year.

My days were spent daydreaming about becoming a Manchester United player until a teacher let a roar at me to bring me back to attention. When I wasn't trapped in school learning Irish, maths, geography and other subjects – which were of little or no use to a Manchester United player – I was outside practicing with a football morning, noon and night.

My daily routine was quite simple back then. It consisted of soccer games in the morning before the bell went, a quick kickabout during our small break, a slightly longer game at big break, and then rushing home as soon as the bell went for an evening of make-believe matches in the garden.

I MUST HAVE been an easy child to rear because I could usually entertain myself most days and I spent most of my time kicking a football against the side of our house. The roof formed a triangle where it met at the end of the house so it was handy for kicking the ball against because it would come back at me in different ways and I'd have to react. Who needs a rebounder when you have the side of a bungalow? You could hear the thump of the ball against the gable wall right up until it got dark and I had to be called inside.

I would practice with both feet too, quickly getting into a rhythm and staying there until I could do it perfectly and without thinking. I still believe that being good with both feet should be a basic requirement for footballers and soccer players these days and it's something I try to drum into my own teams.

My poor mother though, she was nearly driven demented by the sound of the ball smacking her house. But at least she knew where I was and that I wasn't off getting myself into trouble. That would come later!

Eventually though, my one-man aerial bombardment all became too much for Rosaleen, who was afraid of the house falling in on top of her. At some point, two small soccer goals appeared in the garden much to everyone's relief, mine included.

I was now in my element and the house could remain intact as I focused all my energy on trying to hit the crossbars of both goals from a variety of different angles and distances. Practice makes perfect, and it was just as well in my case, because the mother had already threatened to run me back to Athlone on account of all the damage I had done!

The hundreds of hours spent with a football in the garden in Kiltoom was the kind of practice that seems to have become a thing of the past now. It's something you don't really see kids doing anymore.

In fairness, it can be lonely and tedious, and it requires imagination. I watch my two boys at times, and it seems that there are far too many distractions and they require more stimulation.

Some people might see this as a minor thing or just part of modern-day progress, but it has a knock-on effect on young athletes. While our generation was dreaming of scoring winning goals at Wembley and Croke Park outside, youngsters now have FIFA on the PlayStation to give them that feeling, without the muck and sweat.

I didn't have a PlayStation, so I spent my childhood trying to create a stadium atmosphere in that back garden, and I imagined scoring last-minute free-kicks or taking goal-scoring opportunities in big games. While the countryside around our house was silent, thousands of football supporters were cheering me on in my head.

Each kick mattered and I would feel the pressure as I curled the ball into the empty goal. I suppose a modern sports psychologist would call it 'visualisation' nowadays and charge a club or county board a big fee!

Leaving the PlayStation and other distractions aside, practice still requires creativity and for players to have a little bit of imagination. How else would the likes of Dean Rock and David Clifford hone their kicking skills for hours on end?

It's something the former Manchester United and Ireland captain Roy Keane has also spoken about when discussing his time on the FÁS training scheme in Dublin, too. You use your imagination to create an atmosphere or else it's just you on a wind and rain-swept patch of grass in the middle of rural Roscommon. It's easy then to become bored before making excuses and heading back inside to the warmth.

Even though I never gave it the label, visualising became a habit which continued throughout my football career right up until my retirement. I still imagine those high-pressure scenarios when training teams or even when warming up for the odd junior B match nowadays.

Many a cold and wintry night was made that little bit easier by my own imagination.

I'm convinced that the daily practice from childhood paid off and made converting pressure points much easier as I developed into a senior footballer.

« CHAPTER 3 »

I CONSIDER MYSELF incredibly lucky to have been born into a sporting family, and the Dolans were as sports mad as they came! My mother has told me that, as soon as I was able to walk, I had a football in my hands or at my feet.

The Dolans might have been steeped in Gaelic football, but I am not ashamed to admit that soccer was always my first love and to this day I am still a huge supporter of Manchester United.

If I am unfaithful for falling in love with soccer before Gaelic football, then I should probably make another confession before we go any further. Before supporting the Red Devils, I had spent a year following the fortunes of Tottenham Hotspur.

Thankfully, I saw some sense and United became the team for me. Although with the way things have gone in the last few seasons, I might be better off switching back!

I have been a regular visitor to Old Trafford for matches over the years and before Covid-19 hit, a group of us would have made the pilgrimage once or twice a year. Things have obviously changed since March 2020 and like many people, it has given me a new appreciation for watching live sports.

My cross-channel soccer trips started in early childhood and I have great memories of players like Bryan Robson and Norman Whiteside, as well as stocking up on the latest merchandise at the old Manchester United superstore.

AS WELL AS our trips to Manchester there was also a visit to Gelsenkirchen in Germany for Ireland's game against The Netherlands in the 1988 European Championships.

We flew out as part of a St Peter's Football Club tour and that was something I'll never forget. We watched from the terraces as Jack Charlton's 'Boys in Green' were beaten by a late Wim Kieft goal which sent them out of the tournament. The atmosphere among both sets of fans was unbelievable and the desire to become a professional footballer only grew after that.

During the trip we took on a local German club and we fared much better than Ireland did against Gullit and Co. I scored five goals and we won easily, although it wasn't exactly the Bayern Munich youth team we were up against.

We flew home shortly after that game, but there was no sign of a big welcoming parade at Dublin Airport for the young stars of St Peter's. It's a pity we didn't time our return to coincide with Big Jack's Ireland squad, who were given a hero's welcome a couple of days later.

St Coman's also took us to Old Trafford one year and that was something which confirmed I had made the right decision in switching allegiance from Spurs. My cousins Dessie and Gary were part of that trip too and the whole experience, including the atmosphere in the build-up and roar when the red shirts streamed out onto the pitch, really got me hooked on United.

Trips like that at such an young age were always going to give me the soccer bug and added further fuel to my practice sessions in the garden, which by then had transformed into my very own 'Theatre of Dreams'. It was an obsession by then and all other sports, including Gaelic football, came a very distant second.

I still have great memories of our football tours, but I just wish I had kept a hold of some of the souvenirs and United jerseys from the 80s. Those red Adidas strips seem to be coming back into fashion lately and it looks like a set of originals would be worth a few quid on eBay!

MY COUSIN DESSIE, the former Westmeath footballer and current *RTÉ* analyst, was a handy soccer player too. We played together for St Coman's for a couple of years before we both transferred to neighbouring club St Peter's. We split up when I decided to transfer to our bitter local rivals Willow Park at under-16, before moving to Athlone Town for my last two years at underage level.

Dessie and I were fairly close growing up and we both shared an obsession for sport. We would often call out to each other to kick a ball around the garden for a few hours. Garvan and Darren were a bit young to have any real interest in football at that stage and Dessie's brother Gary was the same. Their interest would grow as the years went on, but sport was all that mattered to me and Dessie back then.

I may have been similar in age to my cousin and shared many of the same interests, but at the end of the day, my brothers were my brothers. As the eldest, I always felt a need to watch over Garvan and Darren and protect them. As we got older, and they outgrew me, it became a mutual thing! We have always had each other's backs and we still do to this day.

Like any family, we could go weeks without speaking to each other at home, but as soon as we passed the school gate or the white line of a football pitch, it was a different story. As the old saying goes, 'Blood is thicker than water' and I would always make sure that I was the first man in to back up my brothers at the first sign of trouble.

I am sure it was no different for the likes of Ian and Senan Kilbride, or the Dalys at Pádraig Pearses. The game is not as rough or as wild as it was back in our day, but you will still see Ronan, Niall and Conor backing each other up in any melee. Family is family, even though there are times when they can get on your nerves! The Dolan boys were far from perfect and we had many a row over stupid things growing up but that was quickly forgotten about if someone else decided to take one of us on.

We would grow to see our St Brigid's' teammates as members of our extended family, too. Over the years there have been many brawls and dust ups, especially during ill-tempered challenge games when there was no fear of suspensions. We were involved in some crazy stuff at times and I quickly learned all about my teammates and who could be trusted to jump in and back me up when required. You may have been able to hide out on the pitch but there was nowhere to hide in our dressing-room, or back at the Dolan home house afterwards.

STILL, WE DROVE our mother and sister mad at times with some of the carry-on. One afternoon, Garvan arrived home with a prized trout he had caught down at the lake and we were all admiring it in the kitchen before heading off for a few pints. The trout was left in some newspaper to be cleaned up the next day.

Later that evening we came back from the pub in great form... singing, slagging and messing with each other. It wasn't long though before Garvan was back bragging about his trout.

On and on he went about this thing.

I must have got fed up listening to him because at some point I picked up his new best friend and started moving its mouth while singing and slagging Garvan.

Garvan didn't see the funny side of it though and he went into a bit of a sulk, warning me to put the fish down. I didn't of course and on I went with his new singing and dancing trout.

It all quickly became too much for poor Garv and he turned away in a huff, deciding it was better to just ignore me.

'Jesus, you're no craic Garvan. It's just a bit of codding... get it? Codding?'

Still sulking.

Right, f**k ya then.

SMACK!

I had grabbed the trout by its tail and slapped him full force across the face with it. Bits of muck and trout shite dripped down his chin.

'Ya absolute b*****ks!' He said, and punched the wall in anger, causing a loud crack in his hand.

Kara burst into the kitchen seconds later. She said she feared the worst as she opened the door, expecting to see my lifeless body laid out on the kitchen floor.

Instead, she saw Garvan clutching his hand after breaking it off the wall and me standing there in the middle of the kitchen, laughing my head off, with a filthy trout in my arms.

It was never easy being the only girl in a house full of Dolan men, and I doubt if things are much different these days!

MY FLEDGLING SPORTS career had begun at the age of eight with soccer clubs such as St Coman's, Willow Park and St Peter's FC in Athlone. I was also playing Gaelic football with St Brigid's in Kiltoom and one of my earliest memories of my Brigid's days is of winning the under-12 Roscommon championship.

Despite that early success, however, I was more focussed on soccer at the time and could not have known that that juvenile championship win would be a sign of things to come.

Gaelic football had just failed to capture my imagination and it wasn't long before I turned my attention back to soccer and training sessions and matches in Athlone. One of the main reasons I was finding it difficult to commit solely to Brigid's was that my soccer career had really started to take off, helped by the amount of success we were enjoying at schoolboys' level. We won silverware every year and some of the sides I played with were the talk of the underage leagues across the midlands.

My performances in midfield for Willow Park at under-16 and under-17 eventually attracted the attention of Athlone Town. 'The Town' was the biggest club in the region at that time and supporters still spoke about the 1975 UEFA Cup tie when they had held the mighty AC Milan scoreless at St Mel's Park.

Making the move was an easy decision for me because I saw it as an opportunity to take my first real step towards one day making the grade as a professional footballer.

IN RECENT YEARS, there has been a lot of debate around the pros and cons of playing several different sports as opposed to focusing solely on one. Back then, things were different, and I remember being told that I would have to give up the soccer if I wanted to progress at Gaelic football.

While I continued to juggle both sports into my late-teens, I would warn any young athlete these days that in order to become an elite level player at any sport, you must properly commit to it. It is nearly impossible to continue training at a high level in two different codes and eventually something must give, and that's what happened with me.

STICKING WITH THE soccer was a tough decision, but it was made easier by the fact that I was playing well for Athlone Town and looked to have a bright future in the game. As I developed in my mid-to-late teens, I still believed I could make a living out of it, either in the League of Ireland or in the lower divisions across the water in England.

This wasn't just wishful thinking on my part either because at that time we were more than holding our own in the Dublin and District Schoolboys League, the best underage league in the land. Every week we would come up against the top Dublin schoolboys' clubs such as Cherry Orchard, St Joseph's Boys and St Kevin's. We were well able to compete with them and even completed a famous league and cup double at under-17, beating some of the best teams in the country.

While many young players had drifted away from the game by their late-teens – usually when they started going to parties and stumbled upon the opposite sex – I remained fiercely committed to my dream of signing a professional contract.

By this stage, I was also featuring for an exceptional St Brigid's team. That double commitment each week for training and matches was made even more difficult when I transferred from Athlone Town to Bohemians Reserves. At that time Bohs were managed by Turlough O'Connor. There was no sign of a motorway from Athlone to Dublin back then of course and the games were usually midweek, either at home in the famous Dalymount Park or at other grounds across the city and further afield.

I really loved playing for Bohs and wanted nothing more than to stay on and give it a real go, but it was too much to expect my father to drive up to Dublin each week, and it wasn't long before I was forced to move back to Athlone Town. I didn't know it then, but my reluctant return would lead to the end of my soccer career.

BY THIS TIME, my whole life revolved around sport. Every day I was either training or playing matches. I was lining out for Athlone Town and St Brigid's in the evenings and at weekends, and I was also being targeted as the danger man for the Athlone Community College football team too.

Our school senior team was under local legend Joe Mulvihill and we had a decent side at the time too. We even won some silverware along the way including a Leinster Colleges title. It may have been at a lower grade, but our success was a big deal for us, and I liked to think that it paved the way for the school to go on and win championships at the higher grades.

Between the soccer and the Gaelic football with both St Brigid's and Athlone Community College, there is no doubt I was being overplayed. But there was just no talking to me at that age. I would never have agreed to take a break or allow myself to be rested. It was only a matter of time then before injury or burn-out caught up with me.

In hindsight, it was probably lucky that I picked up a relatively minor injury which forced me to take a break and miss out on playing for a while. Otherwise, I might have ended up getting sick of it and walking away in my late-teens like some of my teammates.

The first sign that something wasn't quite right came following a particularly heavy week with Athlone Town. I could feel this dull pain just below my kneecap. It was nothing I had ever experienced before and because I was afraid I might be told to stop playing, I decided to ignore it and see if it would go away on its own. Pain is part and parcel of playing contact sports and most of the time a little discomfort can be put down to a knock picked up at training or during a match.

When the pain refused to go away after a few days I knew that this was something more serious. The stiffness had become too much, and I was eventually sent for a scan on the injured knee. My father brought me to see the Manchester United physio Jim McGregor in his clinic in Manchester. Jim told me the cartilage was torn.

My worst fears were confirmed when I met with the consultant a few days later. I had seriously damaged the cartilage in the knee through overuse and needed an operation to put it right. An extended spell on the sidelines was the last thing I wanted but I had no choice. Running had become impossible and even walking at that stage was causing discomfort.

I informed Athlone Town of the injury, explaining that it had happened because of wear and tear while representing the club. Their response was not something I had expected. Officials were adamant that it wasn't the club's responsibility to cover the costs of the operation – even though I had spent three years training and playing with them, and was ready to commit my future to soccer at the expense of other sports.

To say I was shocked and hurt would be an understatement. I was also embarrassed that I had been put in this position and that my parents would now have to scrape together the money for the surgery. There was no reasoning with Athlone. It was a very bitter moment and I angrily stormed out of the club, vowing there and then that I would never return.

Though it was difficult to accept at the time, Athlone's attitude to my injury would eventually put a lot of things in perspective for me. There was simply no way that I could continue to play for a club that didn't value me as a player. I took the entire episode as a sign that my future in sport lay elsewhere and it helped me to make the decision to fully commit to Gaelic football and St Brigid's of Kiltoom.

That's not to say that I don't still carry some regrets from that time. If it hadn't been for my falling out with the officials at Athlone Town, there may never have been a Roscommon footballer called Frankie Dolan. I had my heart set on a career in sport and soccer seemed to be the clearest pathway. It was my first love growing up and right up to minor level I could never have imagined that Gaelic football would end up taking its place.

By the time I walked away from St Mel's, I had developed into a decent midfielder and played alongside a few players who would go on to have successful careers in England. My cousin Dessie and I were even offered trials with Reading while still underage but for whatever reason we decided not to travel over. Maybe it was the fear of being homesick. Moving from Athlone to Kiltoom was one thing, but southern England was like another planet!

WHILE I'M HAPPY with how things worked out, I sometimes still think about what might have been had I taken up Reading's offer. There's no doubt in my mind that I could have made it at a decent level over there and perhaps that trial was my golden ticket to something special. I guess we'll never know, but it's human nature to wonder about things like that.

One thing's for sure, you really need the right people around you at that age, to give you advice whenever those opportunities arise. When it came to sport, I made most of my own decisions back then, and I simply wasn't confident enough in myself to uproot and emigrate to the UK. I was still in my teens and I didn't have enough life experience to be able to decide whether something was a good move for me long-term either. I was still just a kid after all.

I'm sure that if I had somebody, say a coach, family member or even a teacher to encourage me to back myself and take a chance, then things may have turned out a lot differently.

My father was a keen supporter no matter what sport I played but I don't think he was the right person to be making decisions for me when it came to moving countries. He was a son of Athlone, who had never ventured too far from the Shannon. I think he would have found it hard to be objective or to put himself in my shoes.

His love for Gaelic football over any other game was also a major obstacle.

He was football-mad and would spend years following Brigid's, Ballymahon and Roscommon – even turning up at training sessions to watch me. He loved travelling around to venues across Ireland to watch matches. Berkshire probably would have been a major let-down for him!

When it came to that fork in the road of my sporting life, I would have benefitted from talking to someone from outside of my immediate family. An outside observer with a knowledge of the world of soccer in England could have quickly assessed whether it was worth my time travelling over for trials. Decisions then could have been made based on my ability and the likelihood that I would go on and earn a few pounds from the game.

I've been extremely fortunate to have a few brilliant people supporting me in my Gaelic football career, particularly in the last few years. Had I known some of these people during my Athlone Town days, I know I would have received sound advice. These people are true friends who have my best interests at heart, and I think they would have supported a move to England to forge a career out of soccer.

I know that there are young starlets in Roscommon, and particularly St Brigid's, who are faced with a similar dilemma now. Players who are offered the opportunity to leave the amateur game of Gaelic football behind and sign contracts with League of Ireland clubs or rugby teams like Connacht. It's a difficult choice to make and I can only offer advice based on my own experience.

If I could do it all again, however, I believe I would have pushed on with soccer. Those offers don't come around again and it's something that you may look back on and regret.

My advice to young players, who are talented in a couple of different sports, is to seek out advice from those who know about the pitfalls in professional sports and particularly those who can offer honest, unbiased guidance.

Looking back, it was very foolish on my part to turn my back on soccer based on a single disagreement with one club. In the long run, I may have suffered more for that decision than Athlone Town.

PART TWO

A New Dream

« CHAPTER 4 »

I STILL HAVE some regrets about the way I walked away from my boyhood dream, but I have no regrets about committing to St Brigid's. It proved to be one of the best decisions I have ever made and one that paid dividends for over 20 years.

While I never really felt like I was part of a community at St Mel's Park, the same could never be said of Kiltoom. The moment I walked into the club I felt like I was part of something bigger than just a Gaelic football team. It felt like I had returned home.

Tony Gavin was over the St Brigid's minor team at the time and I was friendly with his son Mark which made moving on that little bit easier. It didn't take me long to prove that I was fully committed to the club, and it quickly became difficult for me to remember why I ever wanted to play for anyone else.

While I was glad to be back in the heart of my local community, my bitter departure from Athlone Town was an early sign of just how stubborn I could be. It was something that would rear its head from time to time over the following 20 years and counting!

AFTER SURGERY TO repair the damaged cartilage in my knee, I threw myself into representing St Brigid's with even more energy than before. The training was tough, but I really enjoyed it.

I was just 17 at that stage but I was already turning heads at minor level. John Hogan was our captain and leader, while me, John Tiernan and Gerry Dunning were the driving force of the team.

Hogan had developed far quicker physically than the rest of us at that stage. He towered head and shoulders above every one of us. He attended school in Clongowes Wood College in Kildare where he played rugby and I think that sport really took over for him after minor level. He did continue with the club for a couple of years after that though and was even part of our under-21 county success a few years later.

The underage scene certainly wasn't as sophisticated back then. We didn't have the level of coaching or expertise around strength and conditioning and nutrition that young players benefit from these days.

Personalised programmes? Forget it! The team trained together, and it was very much one-size-fits-all with no attention given to any individual work. The only knowledge I had of diet came from my own 'common sense' and the whole idea of recovery sessions wouldn't come into it until much later.

Our training was basic and involved plenty of running before we were let loose on a series of drills with the football. These days there's more purpose to the running drills, or at least I hope there is! Back then though it felt like the physical work was used as a punishment and there certainly wasn't any data to back any of it up.

I never minded the running or the conditioning work, but I've always found it far more enjoyable when there was a football involved. The ball gives the drills more meaning. And sure, if I wanted to be a runner, I would have joined an athletics club!

The best nights were the ones when a coach or mentor would just toss a football in amongst us and shout, 'Play away lads!' It was simple but highly effective and I believed it made proper footballers out of us.

Things have become more organised at training sessions but there is an argument to be made against the increased 'professionalism' these days. Even during Covid-19 lockdowns, lads were expected to be training three or four times a week by themselves without a football. I'm only glad the likes of Zoom and WhatsApp group chats didn't exist when I was a young fella. I think there are some lads who spend more time in the WhatsApp group than they do training with the team. It also makes it easier for the manager to keep an eye on you too!

At the end of the day, I think it is important to remember that Gaelic football is still an amateur sport. It's all gone very technical with analysis and measurements of all kinds used to track a player's progress. There's no doubt that some of this is useful, especially in the older age groups, but it can go too far with younger players.

I've seen it myself at times. Inexperienced coaches trying to prove a point and showing up to sessions with complicated training drills they've seen on the internet. While playing experience isn't essential, it can help when it comes to being able to put yourself in a player's shoes. Some coaches can't see it from the player's point of view and so their drills, and the instructions that go with them, can be a bit suspect.

Now, I think coaches and volunteers should be welcomed from all walks of life. It's a good thing for the sport that coaches with various levels of experience are coming into the game too. It's only by looking at Gaelic football from different perspectives that we will be able to advance it.

From a player's point of view, I have worked with several coaches who brought elements of different sports into the game. This has always been a popular and effective approach in professional sports.

For example, certain tactics and skills from the game of basketball transition very well into Gaelic football. It's no surprise then that former players such as Kieran Donaghy, Kevin Walsh and Liam McHale have used their experience in that sport to great effect when it comes to football.

It's also important to point out that without voluntary coaches coming into the game there would be a shortage of mentors in some areas. Unfortunately, there are many experienced players who choose to hang up their boots and then don't bother their backsides getting involved in mentoring because they feel as though they've already given enough. This puts extra pressure on clubs because it means that they are then forced to take on mentors with less experience or knowledge just to ensure each grade has a management team in place.

It's only since I've gone into management that I've been able to properly observe underage managers and their approach to training. St Brigid's have worked wonders at underage and minor levels in fairness, but I must admit that some of the stuff I've seen among the younger age groups is questionable.

There are times when I've been shocked to see drills and sessions for under-8s and under-10s that are of zero benefit to young players. There were nights when I counted 20 or 30 footballs on the pitch while watching youngsters being forced to run around obstacles and jump over hurdles like an adult team.

Fair enough, they were winning games and weekend blitzes, but imagine if these players were receiving proper football coaching with a ball in their hand from the age of six? It is sometimes easy to forget that these kids aren't playing or practicing as often as they should be when they're at home. For some of them, training is the only opportunity to practice with a football so it's important that the sessions are used to maximum effect.

I think there is so much emphasis on creating athletes nowadays that the skills of Gaelic football are often neglected. Development should start as soon as they sign up with the club and continue right through to adult level. Take it from me, there will be plenty of time for running around obstacles and jumping over hurdles!

BACK IN 1996, we were fortunate to have Tony Gavin as manager and the legendary Roscommon player Danny Murray as a selector alongside Peter McHugh. That breakthrough year would see us enjoy a very impressive run to the county final, where we faced a strong Pádraig Pearses' side.

Our game was the curtain raiser for that year's senior county final between Michael Glavey's and the dominant Roscommon champions Clann na nGael.

Many of the media reports that week would describe our minor showdown for the O'Flynn Cup as far more entertaining than Clann's procession to another county title. There is no doubt that our performance at a sunny Dr Hyde Park that day made our supporters hungry for success at senior level and provided a platform for the following year.

It was a real end-to-end final and thankfully I was in top form, hitting seven points as we ran out 0-13 to 1-8 winners. Tiernan, Hogan, James Kelly and Benny Morris played well that day too and Dara Creaton chipped in with two points as well.

Pearses had been the better side in the first-half and we struggled to get a proper foothold in the game. We did however manage to go in at half-time on level terms which gave us a lot of confidence for the second-half. We were much better after the break. Tiernan scored a brilliant point from out near the '45' and shortly afterwards I scored from even further out to give us a three-point lead.

We thought we were home and hosed at that stage, but Paul Dukes scored a goal for Pearses with about 10 minutes left to level it and set up an exciting finish.

Both sides were guilty of some bad wides in the closing stages which was understandable with the nerves increasing as the ground began to fill for the main event. Thankfully, I was given a simple tap-over free to put us ahead again before wrapping up the title with a point on the full-time whistle.

There was a huge amount of relief when that whistle blew. It was the club's first minor title of any description in over 20 years and so it felt like a monkey off our backs. It was also my first real taste of glory on a Gaelic football pitch, which made it that much sweeter.

The celebrations afterwards are something I won't forget in a hurry either, and in the weeks and months that followed there was a belief that something special was brewing at the club.

Personally, I took great satisfaction from the feeling that I was among the best young players in the county at minor level and it was something that made me proud.

While there would be the odd game for the likes of Cam Celtic after that, there could be no going back to soccer in any serious way. The following year I broke into the Brigid's' senior team as a raw 19-year-old alongside John Tiernan and that was that. I finally felt like Gaelic football was the sport for me. Winning a Roscommon championship at Dr Hyde Park certainly didn't do any harm in that regard!

THERE'S NO DOUBT now that the modern teenager has many distractions, but my teenage years revolved completely around sport. Soccer took up most of my free time from national school until I was around 17 before Gaelic football dominated from then on. Not once did I feel like I was missing out on a social life. I was happiest being a dedicated athlete.

To be honest, I had little interest in the usual teenage pursuits at that stage and I preferred to focus on my development as a footballer.

Lads in my class and even some of my teammates took a slightly different view, however, and began to pay more attention to the opposite sex. While I was busy dedicating every waking hour to improving myself on the field of play, some of my teammates had become a little distracted trying to play a different type of field!

As the years went on, I would learn to appreciate a proper night out with the lads after a tough match, but back then my head was not for turning, and it meant I had no real social life to speak of.

The result of this commitment to a clean life was that I became one of the fittest players on the St Brigid's panel. Training became an addiction, and I couldn't wait to roll up to Kiltoom each evening and test myself against my teammates. I always felt that I had an advantage over lads who had gone out for a few pints after matches, and maybe by cleaning them out in training I was also proving to myself that my 'boring' lifestyle was worth it.

Tough training sessions are a great release for hormonal teenage boys too and I was no different. I didn't mind trudging through the mud on winter evenings because it meant being fit and raring to go for championship action when the summer came around.

Those miserable wintry sessions are where I earned the right to play on warm summer evenings in front of big crowds. The smell of a brand-new O'Neill's football and the adrenaline pumping through my veins as I took on my marker and swung over a score.

That's what I lived and trained for back then and if I had to suffer a few months in the cold each winter then so be it. The pints could wait.

It wasn't until I entered the Roscommon set-up, a few years later in 1999, that I started to loosen up a bit and realise that there was more to life than just training and playing matches. I then started to join my teammates at the bar after matches.

Proof, if any were needed, that Roscommon football could drive any man to drink!

« CHAPTER 5 »

THE PERFORMANCES OF that St Brigid's minor team in 1996 got a lot of people at the club talking and expectation grew for the likes of myself and John Tiernan.

I had already been approached to train with the senior panel that year, during our successful run to the minor final. I was just 17 at the time though and still getting used to the idea of committing myself to Gaelic football. I turned down the opportunity but promised I'd give it more thought after the minor championship.

I remember speaking to my uncle Dessie about it after one of our minor matches and he advised me that there would be plenty of other opportunities to play senior football if that's what I wanted to do. He assured me that I was right to hang on, and who was I to argue with someone who'd played and managed at county level?

There was still a fair bit of pressure to join up with the seniors, but after chatting with Dessie Snr, it felt like a weight had been lifted from my shoulders. He was basically telling me to do what made me happy and not to be trying to please other people at the club.

By that stage, everyone at St Brigid's was desperate for some success at senior level, especially the management team. There were also some senior players who made it clear that they wanted the two minor stars training and playing at senior as soon as possible. I was flattered by all of this but just didn't feel ready to make the step up.

I WAS ENJOYING my football in 1996 and it helped that I was shooting the lights out wherever we played. I had great belief in myself even back then and there was no doubt in my mind that my time would come as a senior player as long as they didn't get sick of waiting for me!

While I had performed brilliantly at minor level for the club, I had still to receive a call-up to any of the county's underage panels. The former Mayo All Star and Roscommon Gaels player Kevin McStay was over the Roscommon minor team at that time but despite my best efforts and some excellent performances, his selectors never picked up the phone.

It hurt at the time I suppose but there wasn't much I could do about it. I just kept my head down and put all my energy into my performances for St Brigid's.

To do this day, and despite winning an All-Ireland club title together in the meantime, I have never managed to pluck up the courage to ask Kevin why I didn't get the nod.

I do think the omission bothered other people at St Brigid's more than me, however. Any rejection I felt only made me even hungrier to pull on the primrose and blue jersey in the years that followed.

Before all that though, I was looking forward to being given the opportunity to prove that I could perform at senior club level.

The senior dressing-room was a daunting prospect for any young player, but I don't remember feeling any butterflies when I took my seat next to the more seasoned players at the club. The atmosphere within that panel was very inclusive and right from the very first session there was plenty of encouragement for John Tiernan and me.

Sure, my markers were suddenly much bigger and stronger, but that only helped me to raise my game and really speed up my development, both as a man and as a player. We were in awe of these guys who had been in battles all over the county and we learned a lot from them in that first year as senior players.

The beautiful thing about the GAA club was that our new teammates were no strangers to us by the time we joined them. I got to know many of them from taking part in senior training sessions over the previous year. There were some real football men in that dressing-room too, men like the Lennons, Tom and Brian, who were always incredibly good to me and still are. It would be no exaggeration to say that those lads are probably the best St Brigid's clubmen in Kiltoom. They were among a group of savage men who always made sure to have your back at the first sign of trouble.

There were others, too, who maybe didn't get the recognition that their ability and commitment deserved. Our wing-forward, Brendan 'Dixie' O'Brien was one of those. Dixie was one of the best footballers I have ever played with. He was just a class operator with a great footballing brain and we always seemed to link up well when playing together.

The success I had enjoyed the year before at minor level meant that I was hugely excited to be taking my place on that team. I felt that I had proven myself at underage level in helping the club to a county title and now the time had come to make the step up to the real thing.

It proved to be a rude awakening.

SEÁN KILBRIDE HAD persuaded Mayo man John O'Mahony to take charge of the senior team that year. John had already achieved legendary status after guiding the provincial underdogs Leitrim to a Connacht title just three years before. He would also go on to even greater things with Galway in 1998, so it was fair to say we had him at the peak of his powers.

John was a manager who commanded the respect of the entire dressing-room the moment he walked in. It's still a wonder to me that he was never hounded to take the Roscommon job.

The first rule for John was that you worked hard, and he ran us like obedient dogs that year. He was helped by the fact that there was such a great buzz around the place. We had a close bond and there was a positive feeling in the camp which everyone had bought into. Good morale was to be important that year because the training itself was far different to anything we had ever experienced before. Forget about running around a pitch in Kiltoom, our new manager brought us up to the army firing range in Carnagh where they had obstacle courses and climbing walls. The running drills were more like torture and I still get the odd flashback and cold sweats watching *Ireland's Fittest Family*!

A few weeks of training at the military range though and the body and mind became hardened, so by the time the summer came around we were ready to go to war ourselves.

I may have been a natural forward, but I would never have described myself as a natural athlete. Running up and down the pitch and covering every blade of grass was never my thing, but I was the most prolific finisher on our St Brigid's minor team and always put in a shift.

From a young age, I thrived under pressure too and that was something that would continue throughout my career. I enjoyed the tension around big matches and was happy to be working under a demanding manager like John O'Mahony.

I never really had much interest in the likes of league games with the club or the FBD League with Roscommon. The National Football League games also failed to really inspire me back then. I lived for the high stakes of championship matches when winning really mattered. The higher the stakes, the more I enjoyed it.

I've always loved knockout championship football and one of the silver linings of lockdown 2020 was getting to see teams play in that format. The games were unpredictable, and teams went hell for leather... knowing if they lost, they were gone.

That to me is beautiful. Just like the old Roscommon championship and then of course Connacht and All-Ireland club championships. No second chances. No trying to lift yourself for a qualifier. If you're gone... you're gone! The 2020 knockout All-Ireland championship really captured the imagination of supporters and they are the games I miss playing in the most.

From the age of 17 right up until my retirement, those 'do-or-die' matches really set my pulse racing. The big Roscommon matches in front of 20,000 or even 30,000 people at Dr Hyde Park. Supporters crammed into the ground, desperate for us to win. Their happiness, and in some cases, their whole summer, resting on our shoulders.

I loved that feeling, that expectation. It was the closest thing to a drug for me. I was right at home in that pressure cooker atmosphere, especially when the national media were in town and the county's pride was on the line.

IT HAD BEEN 28 years since St Brigid's had won the Roscommon senior championship, but with John O'Mahony at the helm we finally managed to bridge that gap in 1997.

There had also been hard work done behind the scenes and Sean Kilbride and Marty McDermott deserve great credit for that. Our underage structure was beginning to take shape at this point and that would pay dividends, both that year and for many years after.

O'Mahony's appointment as manager was also a great coup for the club and the timing couldn't have been better for young players like me and John Tiernan, who were just breaking into the team.

He not only trained us hard, but he also used his great motivational skills to give us the belief needed to end our long wait for a county title. At our very first team meeting at the start of the year, John produced this team poster with 'St Brigid's County Champions 97' written on it.

'Lads, this is going to be the year,' he told us. He was adamant that the group of players sitting in front of him would bring home the Fahey Cup.

It was basic sports psychology compared to what players experience nowadays but it was enough to spark a reaction in us. The place was buzzing. Lads were itching to go training even in the depths of winter and at many of those sessions we could have around 30 players togged. We all bought into John's process and I don't think he could have any complaints about our commitment that year.

The gruelling training sessions and John's straightforward methods of getting lads fired up really stood to us in the latter stages of the championship. We had also developed a staying power that proved too much for most of our opponents.

THAT YEAR WE ended the St Brigid's' famine in the best possible way, by beating our fierce rivals and neighbours Clann na nGael in the county final. Clann had dominated Roscommon and Connacht since the 80s but there was a sense in Kiltoom and other parts of the county that their power was waning. They had dished out hammerings to various Brigid's' teams in the past, but we believed our time had come.

We had played well throughout the championship that year with a team that was peaking just at the right time. The fact that Johnno had us in the best shape of our lives also gave us great confidence. There was a belief among the players in that dressing-room that no other Roscommon team would beat us for fitness.

The final itself was a relatively low-scoring game and it's fair to say that Clann were not at their best. Paul McManus went off injured following a goalmouth scramble midway through the second-half and there is no doubt that helped us. Paul had unfortunately ruptured the cruciate ligament in his knee and there was a huge delay to the match which would lead to a nerve-racking eight minutes of injury-time at the end.

The incident undoubtedly had an effect on some of Paul's teammates and Clann were also forced to play on with 14 having used all their substitutes.

Our very own Captain Marvel Tom Óg O'Brien was named Man of the Match for his selfless display while I finished as our top scorer with four points in a 1-8 to 0-8 win. Though there was evidence in my play that I was still developing in terms of shot selection and composure.

I did get the score of the game from out near the sideline but I also missed a couple of easy chances, including a simple 25-yard free. It had been a terrific debut year in senior football, but it was clear that there was still plenty of room for improvement.

The other young star of the St Brigid's team, John Tiernan grabbed our goal that day, and showed just how desperate we were to beat our neighbours in the process. As John reached to get his fist to the ball, he smacked his head off the crossbar and ended up in the net. It looked painful, but he certainly wasn't going to be the only man with a headache in Kiltoom that week!

Sitting in the dressing-room afterwards, there was a feeling of relief that we had finally managed to get that county title monkey off our back. There were fantastic scenes too and it was great to see men like our captain Tom Óg so happy. Club legend Gerry O'Malley arrived into the dressing-room and went around each player shaking their hand. That was a lovely moment, and we were delighted to be able to hand him the cup after such a long wait.

I was still a long way from the legendary status of the great man, and I was still finding my feet as a senior footballer, which probably showed in the dressing-room interview I gave to the local papers that afternoon.

'Frankie, tell us about that Maurice Fitzgerald effort out near the sideline in the second-half?' a reporter asked.

'I had practiced a few things in training, but the wind brought that one in,' I told them, slightly uneasy about being compared to the Kerry legend.

Truth be told, I was a little bit embarrassed by the attention, particularly with the other lads, who had soldiered for years, celebrating just a few feet away. That day was all about St Brigid's as a club rather than Frankie Dolan or any other individual player. I was just delighted to be part of it.

The celebrations continued back at the clubhouse in Kiltoom that night and right throughout the week across the parish. I was still completely focused on my fitness at that stage, so I managed to keep a clear head while the rest of the Green and Red Army celebrated and suffered as one.

At that time, I was working for the ESB. I joined straight after school and luck would have it that my first day on the job was just after we had won the county final. Another reason to avoid the celebrations!

While I hadn't been drinking beer on the Sunday and Monday with the rest of my teammates, I would have to deal with a hangover of a different kind in my new job that week.

The ESB had us working in 'gangs', which were basically just groups of workers assigned to one area and usually working out of the same vehicles. And guess who happened to be in my gang on my first day on the job? None other than Clann na nGael manager John Dowling!

'Mornin' John,' I shouted cheerfully with my county medal hanging out of my arse pocket. A great start to my career with the ESB!

The rivalry between ourselves and Clann is probably the fiercest in Roscommon football, both at underage level and senior ranks.

Despite all the battles over the years, I can still count at least one good friend from the Johnstown club in Johnny Dunning. We played together with Roscommon and we're cut from the same cloth. It also helps that neither of us really cares about the rivalry between the two clubs. We'd rather focus on our own game and do whatever we can to help our respective teams win.

While Brigid's managed to gain the upper hand during my time as a player, Clann were never shy in mentioning their great successes of the 80s and 90s. The rivalry was much worse back then for St Brigid's as the men from Johnstown regularly handed down heavy beatings to their poor neighbours from Kiltoom. Those heavy defeats had left a very bitter taste in some mouths.

THE RIVALRY WAS always in the back of our minds and indirectly led to Clann being relegated from Division One in the Roscommon league in 2006.

We had to play Roscommon Gaels in a match in Ballyforan. It was a meaningless game for us, but the Gaels were still involved in a relegation scrap with Clann. If the Gaels won, they would stay up so, for once, Clann were hoping that we'd do the business that night in Ballyforan.

Sadly, for Clann, even though we put up a good fight, my finishing let us down in the closing stages and we let the Gaels off the hook.

The game was in its last few minutes with the Gaels leading by two points when I went through one-on-one with their goalkeeper. Normally in that situation I'd put man and ball through the back of the net to give us the lead.

This time though something felt different. I don't know whether it was because I felt sorry for the young lad in goal or what, but I tapped the ball over the bar and took my point.

I swear, it was only when I was running out the field that Clann's predicament crossed my mind. The Roscommon Gaels manager Johnny Foley hadn't forgotten though and he gave me a big thumbs up from the sideline.

The Gaels played well that night and they were back on the attack with just two minutes left. One of their players was dragged down near the square and the referee Ollie Kelly awarded them an easy free for a two-point lead. There were reports afterwards that one or two of the lads on our bench had jumped up and appealed for Ollie to award a penalty, but I wouldn't know if that was true. The Gaels went on to win the match anyway and Clann were relegated.

I'M GLAD TO say that since our county final win in 1997 it's been mostly St Brigid's who have been on top in the rivalry. Believe it or not, as a player I have only ever been on the losing side of the fixture once in my entire Brigid's career.

That defeat arrived in my last game in 2015, and despite all the success I have enjoyed, it still left a sour taste in the mouth.

It's strange how things can come full circle sometimes. My Brigid's' senior career had really taken off in 1997 after Paul McManus had left the field early and my own time as a player would end in similar circumstances. Referee Paul Daly black-carded me after just 23 minutes of the Roscommon championship semi-final in 2015 before sending Garvan off just 11 minutes later. It was a miserable end to a glorious 20 years with St Brigid's, and an excellent young Clann team ran out winners by two points.

I wasn't to know how it would all pan out back in the summer of 1997 as we celebrated our first county title since 1969 and prepared to take on the rest of the province in a bid to replace the mighty Clann as 'Kings of Connacht'.

We were due to play the reigning Connacht champions Knockmore in Kiltoom on the Sunday after the county final. That game was given very little thought as the celebrations continued right into the middle of the week.

There were a few lads who stayed away from the pints and parties, but others were, understandably, determined to drag the winning feeling out for as long as they could.

Dolan the designated driver was busy that week ferrying lads around the parish. I didn't mind it because I was just 19 at the time and not yet interested in the drink. Players like our captain Tom Óg and Padraig Kilcommons though were determined to enjoy the success after years of watching Clann dominate.

Myself and one of the lads said we'd drop out to Athleague were Tom Óg lived at the time, so we jumped into my brand new Volskwagen Golf and away we went to Waldron's Pub.

You must understand that back then you wouldn't have been setting your stall out to win a Connacht title or an All-Ireland, especially after you'd just ended a long wait without a county title. We were enjoying our moment and for some of those lads it had been a long time coming.

When it came time to head home that night, we all piled back into the Golf where, inside, poor Padraig Kilcommons was snoring away. Padraig slept right through all the slagging and laughing.

The following Sunday came around far too quickly for some when Knockmore arrived for our Connacht showdown. Before travelling to Kiltoom that day we completed a warm-up at Curraghboy National School. We then piled onto the bus and made our way to our home pitch with rebel songs blaring and some of the boys singing and dancing in the aisle.

It was a surreal sight ahead of a big match and showed how little we thought of the Connacht championship. We were happy enough with our win in Roscommon that year. Knockmore though had bigger prizes in their sights after being denied by Crossmaglen in that year's All-Ireland club final at Croke Park.

It was mayhem on our team bus that morning; you'd swear we were heading back to Waldron's for another night out!

Anyone with any sense would have lumped money on the Mayo champions to hammer us, which they did, running out easy eight-point winners.

Despite our tame exit from the Connacht championship, it was still a great year for the club and John O'Mahony deserves huge credit for the job he did. He gave us a great boost and drove us on to end the club's long barren spell. He went on to manage Galway the following year and the rest, as they say, is history.

WHILE JOHN WENT on to great things with Galway, it would be eight years before we got our hands on another county title. There was a misguided belief among some of those involved in the club that the dam had burst with that win over Clann and years of success lay before us.

In reality, a number of key players from that victorious county final team of 1997 were running out of road in terms of their playing careers and most would depart from the panel over the following years.

Men like Benny O'Brien, Tom Óg, the Lennons and Padraig Sugrue, to name just a few, would soon ride off into the sunset, having served the club so well and for so long. It was always going to be a tall order to replace such fine players and there was certainly a leadership void in the team in the years that followed.

Rather than being the start of a golden era for the club, our victory over Clann in 1997 proved to be a false dawn and there would be more championship pain in the years that followed.

The older lads must have known something we youngsters didn't, and events over the next few years would prove they had been right to milk the celebrations for all they were worth!

PART THREE

Primrose and Blue

« CHAPTER 6 »

THE MAJOR SILVERWARE may not have been flowing at club level from 1997 on, but between 1998 and 2001 I enjoyed a couple of highly successful years in the primrose and blue of Roscommon.

Being overlooked for the Roscommon minor team really spurred me on for St Brigid's and it wasn't long before I was getting the call for other underage county panels. I first started training properly with the Roscommon senior panel in the summer of 1998 and the manager Gay Sheerin brought me in for a couple of training games around that time too. There were nights when I was just cleaning up, and the likes of Francie Grehan would be getting on to me to properly commit to it.

The Connacht championship was in full heat at that stage and I was just coming in for training sessions between games. I felt I more than held my own, but I was reluctant to give up my summers just yet! I had come to the attention of the under-21 selectors by then and that was enough for me.

Consultations I had with my uncle Dessie once again confirmed my feeling that I was right to bide my time. I was still quite young, and I was confident the opportunity would come again. I still supported the Rossies throughout 1998, of course, and remember watching the Connacht final against Galway in Tuam. Like most Roscommon supporters that day, I felt we were crucified by the referee, who awarded Galway a soft free in the dying minutes of the game.

To make matters worse, it was a dreadful day, and we were all soaked to the skin on the terraces. Galway managed to nick a draw and there was a feeling among the supporters as we made our way back to Roscommon that our chance had gone.

I watched the replay at a friend's house in Athlone. I remember it was a beautiful day for football, and he was outside kicking a ball against a wall while I sat inside watching Roscommon struggle. I've never been a very good armchair supporter and it wasn't long before I was outside with the football too.

Galway were deserving winners and would go on to win the All-Ireland that year, but I saw nothing in the two games that convinced me I couldn't play at senior county level. By the end of that summer, I had my mind made up that the time had come to fully commit to the county panel. I knew what I was letting myself in for. I knew all the players and backroom lads by then too which made it even easier to take the plunge.

THERE WERE A couple of absolute lunatics on that Roscommon panel at the time and a real old school feel to the way things were done. There was also a proper drinking culture among those players and that was something I hadn't really been exposed to before. It was going to be a steep learning curve for a young, innocent lad, who had been living like a monk up to that point!

Drinking and nights out were still new hobbies to me. I didn't have the interest in my teens which meant that I was a latecomer to the party. I remember having about three or four pints at my debs and arriving home early. Imagine! Sport really dominated my life back then so I suppose I had a lot of catching up to do.

The presence of Francie and Tommy Grehan, Clifford McDonald, Mick 'Mixer' Ryan, Nigel Dineen and a few more in that Roscommon dressing-room meant it was the perfect place for a green newcomer like me to grow up – both on and off the pitch.

Gay Sheerin had stayed on as manager following a promising run to the Connacht final in 1998. He was unlucky not to have guided Roscommon to the Connacht title. Galway got out of jail and needed that replay to see us off, with Michael Donnellan's goal enough to finally get them over the line. Those were the fine margins between agony and ecstasy, and Gay made sure we understood that when we returned for 1999.

Gay always put an emphasis on fitness work and he was also very organised.

The panel used to meet up and train at Custume Barracks in Athlone with a guy called Paul Gilligan. Before strength and conditioning became a buzz phrase in Gaelic football, Paul was there putting us through our paces. Not that we appreciated his expertise at the time when he was running us all over Athlone!

The parade square in the barracks is a place that will live long in our memories. Our drill sergeant Paul ordered us to sprint up and down it until we were ready to drop.

He also had us running out by Baylough some Tuesday evenings. It was during one of those runs that we were greeted by the sight of my best mate James Comiskey enjoying a pint of cider and a smoke outside Ward's Pub. I'll never forget how he just stood there with a big stupid grin on his face shouting at us.

'Ye're doing the county proud!' he roared, as he took a drag on his cigarette.

IT WAS A much simpler time in Gaelic football, when tactics and 'systems' weren't really a big part of the game. Gay certainly wasn't a man to analyse video or overdo it on tactics. It was very much a case of winning your personal battles and doing the right thing with the ball. Fitness was vital to him though and Gay never wanted it said that his team had been outrun. The approach was less about science and more to do with honest, hard graft. Hard work and fitness will only get you so far though and a talented Mayo team hammered us at MacHale Park in the semi-finals that year. To say it was disappointing would be an understatement after all the progress we had made under Gay the year before. There's no excusing an 11-point drubbing at the hands of your fiercest rivals, though.

Our championship had started so well too and we were comfortable against Leitrim in the quarter-finals. Mayo gave us a badly needed reality check and went on to beat Galway in the final.

While the year came to a disappointing end with the senior team, I did enjoy provincial success with the under-21s. We had a strong team that featured the likes of Stephen Lohan, Gerry Lohan, John Tiernan, Gary Cox, John Whyte and John Hanly. It was a fun team to watch and we gave supporters some great days out that year, before beating Sligo with six points to spare in the Connacht final. It was a great confidence boost and a few of the lads would go on to become important senior players in the years that followed.

As part of the celebrations that week, we went up to Carrick-on-Shannon to celebrate Kilmore man Brendan Bourke's 21st birthday. We even took the JJ Fahy Cup along with us for what turned out to be a wild night.

I remember we woke up the following morning the worse for wear and, as we were getting our things together, there was a mad panic when we realised the silverware had gone AWOL. Lads were frantically trying to retrace their steps, but there was no sign of it anywhere. To this day, we don't know where it went but, thankfully, it did turn up safe and sound about a month later. JJ Fahy must have been having an even better night of it than we were!

WE HAD NO fear of anyone that year and so we remained quietly confident even when drawn against the mighty Kerry in the All-Ireland semi-finals. The game was down for Ennis, and the weather was quite warm for that time of year. The conditions were perfect for football. Our only problem was that from the moment we left Roscommon absolutely nothing went right.

We had stopped at the Auburn Lodge before the match for some food and when we went to rejoin the queue of traffic to Cusack Park, our bus broke down. There was no air conditioning – the windows did not open either – and so we sat there for a few minutes, baked alive in the heat. After a while and with no sign of the bus moving again, we jumped into supporters' cars and made our way to the ground. Some of the lads even managed to leave their gear bags behind them on the bus such was the panic that day. Things went from bad to worse when we did finally reach Cusack Park. John Whyte pulled his hamstring after just 10 minutes and the rest of us were already dead on our feet.

When the ball was thrown in, Gerry Kelly took it upon himself to try and even things up. Gerry was a seriously talented boxer and he decided he'd deck the great Tomás Ó Sé off the ball. Gerry would later report that he knew we were in big trouble when Ó Sé took the punch and then just laughed in his face!

Kerry beat the amateur boxers and worn-out footballers from Roscommon that day and went on to contest the final against Westmeath. Of course, the Lake County beat them and became All-Ireland champions thanks to the efforts of a corner-forward called Dessie. I don't know whether that made our defeat easier or harder to take! Our fun representing the county didn't end with defeat in Ennis because now that our run was over, there was a night out to be had. A few of us finished the long, hot day in the popular Queen's Nightclub. When closing time came and there was nowhere else to go, we decided to head back to the Auburn Lodge to see if we could bunk in with some of the supporters.

It was about four in the morning when we arrived at the entrance to the reception. The place was in complete darkness. We took turns trying the doors.

The hotel appeared to be locked up for the night.

The following details are a bit hazy, but we eventually found a way into a function room and decided to bed down there for the night rather than roaming the halls knocking on random doors. At one stage the night porter walked into the function room and we had to duck in behind the long curtains that ran from one end of the room to the other. We ended up sleeping there just in case he decided to come back!

We woke up that Sunday morning and had breakfast and a few pints before getting lifts home from the supporters who had stayed there legally the night before. All in all, it was ideal preparation for the Roscommon senior team!

IT MIGHT HAVE been all fun and games with the underage teams, but things went from bad to worse in the year of the millennium for senior manager Gay Sheerin and his tenure came to an end following an embarrassing 1-13 to 3-6 defeat to Leitrim in the Connacht semi-finals. There were no excuses, we had been given an easy route to the final, having crushed London 4-18 to 0-10 in the quarter-finals.

We were cruising to victory against Leitrim too and probably believed we had the match won at half-time. They must have sensed our complacency in the second-half because they tore into us as soon as they came storming out from the dressing-room. When the momentum of a match shifts like that it can be almost impossible to get it back and our disastrous second-half performance meant that we were dumped out of the championship, and deservedly so.

I still struggle to explain it really.

Myself and Gerry Lohan had a field day in the first-half and there should have been more than just a goal and a point between us. It was all too easy, but if we had been a bit more ruthless we could have had three more goals going in at the break.

I don't want to be unkind to Leitrim, who stuck at it and clawed back a seven-point deficit, but it was unforgivable from our point of view. The feeling of shame as the Leitrim supporters streamed onto the Hyde Park pitch that day is something that never leaves me. We skulked back to the dressing-room in the rain.

The place was like a morgue.

Poor Gay Sheerin was heartbroken afterwards, but the fault lay entirely with the players. The attitude was all wrong in that second-half and Leitrim made us pay. It is no exaggeration to say that it was perhaps a bigger shock than their Connacht championship win in 1994.

There was great sympathy for Gay in that Roscommon dressing-room afterwards. He had put so much into it and had done everything he possibly could to deliver success to the county. A defeat to Leitrim is unacceptable for Roscommon, however, and he didn't have to wait too long before the knives were sharpened for him.

Knowing Gay as I do, I think he was more concerned with the fact that he hadn't brought the Connacht title home rather than any personal disappointment he experienced. There was never any bullshit with Gay, you knew exactly where you stood with him. I'll always have a special affinity towards him for handing me my senior debut, and for those first two years in the primrose and blue.

Throughout my time with Roscommon, Gay was the only Roscommon man who was given a fair crack of the whip, in my opinion. He understood Roscommon football and had his heart set on leading us to glory. It meant a lot to him, more so than for some other managers who arrived from outside the county during that time.

GAY WAS BACK in the headlines in 2017 after he criticised the Roscommon management team while commentating on *Shannonside FM*. He hit out at the fact that Kevin McStay and Liam McHale were in charge of the team by then and said he didn't like seeing Mayo men on the sideline for Roscommon. The comments caused a bit of a storm at the time, and Kevin refused to speak to the radio station for a while afterwards.

Playing devil's advocate, I could understand what Gay meant but I do think he got carried away and crossed a line. I was glad to hear that both men have since made up and I wouldn't have expected anything less from either.

While he was an All Star for Mayo, Kevin had been living in Roscommon for over 30 years and had been involved with a number of clubs and underage teams. Liam is also a great fella and both men have given a lot to Roscommon football.

I don't think what Gay said in the heat of the moment was very fair on either man. He is, however, extremely passionate about his county and was one of the best goalkeepers around during his playing days.

TO MY MIND, there were plenty of good men who would have been well able to manage the Roscommon senior team during my playing career but who were never given the chance.

Maybe I'm wrong, but I think certain players, like yours truly, would have been given a fairer chance if the manager was from Roscommon or had a proper connection to the county, like Kevin. Managers arriving from outside a county want to lay down a marker from the outset and that can mean alienating players they see as potential troublemakers. I'm man enough to admit that there are times when I may have fallen into that category!

John Maughan's reign is a prime example. I didn't feature at all in John's first year in charge. I don't think that would have happened had someone like Fergal O'Donnell got the job. I think Fergie would have had a chat with certain players. He would have wanted the best players in the county available for selection, rather than arriving in and looking to stamp his authority straight away.

I wasn't the only player affected by this. There were others over the years who were entitled to feel hard done by when it came to Roscommon selections.

In some ways it's easier for an 'outsider' to come in and lay down the law because it's not their county and therefore they've no real loyalty to anyone. In most cases, they are basing their opinion of players on what they see during televised games and what they hear in the media.

If I was taking the Roscommon job, or any job for that matter, I would want my best players involved. Everyone would be given a chance to either impress me or let me down.

It's important to remember too that players react differently to certain managers and management styles. Some thrive under strict rules and authority while others need to be cut some slack. It also helps to treat players like adults and trust them to perform when it matters, too.

As Gay's tenure came to an end, we knew that we had let him down.

There would be opportunities for the players to prove our detractors wrong but for Gay, time had run out and it would be a few years before a Roscommon man was handed the reins again.

« CHAPTER 7 »

THE COUNTY BOARD went west for their next appointment and Galway man John Tobin was ratified in 2000 after Sheerin had stepped down. John, or 'Toby' as he was known, freshened things up by bringing Francie Grehan's father Frank and Jimmy Finnegan (RIP), as well as Brian Talty in with him.

We had a couple of good years with Toby, and the highlight of course was winning the Connacht title in 2001, having beaten Galway in Tuam in the semi-final and Mayo with a Gerry Lohan goal in injury-time at the end of the final at Dr Hyde Park.

Not only were we successful in Connacht but we also reached a couple of National League semi-finals too which suggested we were heading in the right direction. Despite all of that, I think Toby could be considered slightly unfortunate with the number of injuries and suspensions we had to endure during his time at the helm.

Whereas Gay Sheerin had focused on fitness, Toby brought a more technical eye to the set-up. He was more of a coach than a manager and that was evident from the great work he had done with young players in Tuam. There wasn't really any coaching going on at that time so in that way Toby was a bit of a revelation. He introduced us to a lot of skills' work, but in typical Gaelic football fashion he also ran the arse off us when we needed it!

He was also very shrewd and surrounded himself with top-class coaches.

Des Ryan was his strength and conditioning coach, for example. Des was with Connacht Rugby at the time and up until recently was Head of Sports Medicine for Arsenal Football Club in London. The training was a major step up compared to what we had been used to before and it paid instant dividends in that summer's championship.

Before that, however, we impressed in the National League which was played from November 2000 to April 2001. Losing just two games in Division 1A, we finally bowed out in the semi-finals as Mayo went on to win it. It was a good warm-up for us ahead of the Connacht championship and proof that Roscommon could compete.

THAT SUMMER, New York were put to the sword in the quarter-finals of the championship at Dr Hyde Park. I was in excellent form and scored a couple of goals in a 3-13 to 1-9 win. That was New York's last visit to Ireland before the 9/11 terror attacks, which made travelling back and forth far more difficult. I do believe though that by playing New York's championship fixture in the Big Apple it allows them to be more competitive, as we've seen in recent years. It's also a great trip away for supporters from Connacht and, more importantly, it offers fundraising opportunities for smaller counties too.

Our convincing win over New York set up a semi-final with Toby's native Galway in Tuam and his cute side really came to the fore in the build-up to that game. He agreed to do an interview with RTÉ on the Friday and gave nothing away in terms of team selection or our preparations.

He even played down our chances to such an extent that you'd swear we hadn't a hope, and that maybe the poor people in Roscommon were even lucky to have a team. His mind games were so effective that I nearly believed him myself!

I don't know whether the interview influenced the Galway team or not, or whether it led to a bit of complacency within their ranks, but they couldn't live with us that day in Tuam. We played some of our best football under Toby in that semi-final.

Michael Donnellan, our tormentor in 1998, was one of Galway's prime danger men and so our players came together before the game to discuss what to do about him. There was total agreement among the senior players in our pre-match huddle.

'That fella can't be allowed any space or time on the ball.

'Close him... drag out of him...

'SMASH HIM... whatever it takes just stop him...

'Or... he'll destroy us!'

Now, we would never go out to injure a player or anything like that. You'd just let him know that if he takes a second too long on the ball, he'll be hit hard. I've come in for similar attention over the years and when it's done right it can slow you down or cause you to play within yourself.

Donnellan was a classy footballer and we felt we had no other option but to set out our stall to stop him. We doubled up on him, hit him late at times, and generally just tried to rough him up or slow him down. Being the footballer he was though, he responded by scoring an outrageous point in the first-half before our man marking eventually began to take its toll.

We celebrated a famous 2-12 to 0-14 win at the full-time whistle, but Galway would use the pain of that defeat to spur them on to All-Ireland glory later that year as the great John O'Mahony worked his magic once again.

AS THRILLED AS I was, our win had come at a cost as I injured my shoulder while competing for possession with Tomás Mannion. I had managed to get out in front but as I went to turn past him, I lost my footing and fell to the ground heavily. Straight away I felt a pop followed by the worst pain I have ever experienced in my life.

I could only watch from the turf as Galway turned over possession and went on the attack. Luckily for us, Kieran Comer drove a gilt-edged goal chance over the bar and the lads were able to hang on.

I made my way off the pitch in agony, with little hope of playing any part in the Connacht final against Mayo. My worst fears were confirmed later that week when I was told that the shoulder would need surgery.

THERE ARE TIMES when my stubbornness works to my advantage though and in the weeks leading up to the Connacht final it was in overdrive.

I had been told that provided I completed intense rehabilitation exercises each day, I could delay the surgery until after the championship. I didn't need to be told twice! I gritted my teeth and worked the shoulder as much as I could as we prepared for the arrival of Mayo.

I was glad I did.

Injured shoulder or not, I was proud to be part of one of the most exciting days of sport Roscommon town has ever experienced.

We were full of confidence after our win in Tuam but winning our 21st Connacht title would still mean beating a team that had hammered us just the year before. Mayo's record against Roscommon down through the years speaks for itself and in 2001 they had a strong, physical, and above all skilful team… players like Trevor Mortimer, David Brady, Ciaran McDonald and Noel Connelly. It was a serious team on paper and they rarely disappointed in the flesh either.

The atmosphere on that summer's day in Dr Hyde Park was the best I have ever experienced. It was a balmy day, and you could feel the heat and the energy coming off the crowd. The place was packed; it was rocking and there wasn't a breath of air to be had anywhere on that pitch.

The excitement had started before the match. We had finished our preparations in The Abbey Hotel and decided we'd walk to the Hyde for the match. There was no need for a Club Rossie bus that day!

We strolled down the Circular Road onto the County Home Road as one, mingling with supporters on the way. There were handshakes and slaps on the back, and we could sense how badly the people of Roscommon wanted us to win. Mayo lifting the Nestor Cup at our expense and in our own backyard was unthinkable and our supporters weren't shy in reminding us of that. We were relaxed though, and the walk made it clear to us that at least we weren't going into battle alone.

I DON'T REMEMBER feeling nervous in the dressing-room that day, but I was almost overwhelmed by the noise and the colour as we paraded around the pitch before throw-in. The primrose and blue and the roar from the scoreboard end, it was like having our very own Hill 16 in Roscommon. The supporters were packed along the terraces and the main stand. The official attendance was something like 28,000 but there seemed to be more people there that day and the noise they made was deafening.

The game itself was very tight all the way through and that just added to the occasion. The first-half was low on quality as both sides kept giving possession away. It may have been end-to-end, but it was brainless stuff at times with no real composure from either side.

The second-half was a big improvement. While there were still mistakes on both sides, it was a much better spectacle at least. It could have all ended so differently for us that day and I'm sure there were plenty of worried Roscommon supporters when Mayo substitute David Nestor blasted past Derek Thompson in injury-time.

There were desperate attempts to stop David Brady, another Mayo substitute, as he rampaged towards goal but his handpass found Nestor, who made no mistake from close-range before celebrating in front of our supporters at the graveyard end. We had missed plenty of chances and it had begun to feel like just another one of those days.

WE HAD BEEN trailing early in the game, but our captain Fergal O'Donnell and Seamus O'Neill just wouldn't take defeat lying down. Michael Ryan was another warrior that day and Gerry Lohan was clinical in front of goal when it mattered.

I chipped in with three points of my own, including a nice finish in the first-half when Gerry won back possession and found me lurking about 30 yards from goal. I had been relatively quiet up to that point as the long balls were pumped in towards Gerry and his brother Stephen. Perhaps a little more composure could have made the dying minutes more bearable for everyone!

We showed our fighting spirit that day though and, more importantly, kept our promise to those supporters we had met on the way to the Hyde earlier that afternoon. It had been a brave fight-back from our point of view, after we had let a two-point half-time lead slip. Mayo came out all guns blazing in the second period and when Clifford McDonald was sent off, we looked to be in big trouble. Mayo's discipline let them down though and Ray Connelly was sent off following an off the ball incident involving yours truly.

Poor Ray. It was a simple case of mistaken identity.

Their goalkeeper Peter Burke was the one who should have been given his marching orders. It started as a Mayo tag-team when Burke came out of his goal and threw a hand in my direction, while at the same time Connelly pushed me. It was innocent stuff in fairness, but I went down clutching my jaw and the umpires called referee Seamus McCormack over for a chat.

Connelly was shown the red card, but I had recovered from the 'frightening and unprovoked' attack at that stage and was pleading his case to McCormack.

'You've got the wrong man ref. It was that Burke fella!'

The referee didn't pass any heed and Connelly didn't look too impressed with me either as he made his way off the pitch.

It would later turn out that McCormack hadn't seen the incident initially and if you watch it back on YouTube it's the umpire wearing the glasses who seemed to be making his mind up for him. This was in an era before they were sponsored by Specsavers I suppose!

Connelly's sending off was overturned after the match, but he had been performing well so it was a huge boost for us to see him leave the field. We continued to create chances and always believed that it was only a matter of time before we made them pay.

It was their goalscoring hero David Nestor who made the mistake which led to Gerry Lohan's winning goal. Brady had played a clever ball out towards him in space and for whatever reason he tried to flick it on instead of catching it. The ball went out of play and Mayo just seemed to switch off.

Johnny Whyte drove the sideline ball up the field towards Johnny Dunning, who made an excellent catch before drawing a foul.

Johnny then took a quick free to Denis Gavin, who in turn found Gerry Lohan on the edge of the Mayo square. 'Junior' kept his cool, dummied two defenders… cut back onto his left and smacked home a cool finish to win it for us. Not bad composure for the fifth minute of injury-time!

Thinking back on that moment now, he's lucky he found the net. Myself and Francie Grehan were in much better positions at the time and would have taken turns killing him had he missed!

If the roles had been reversed, and I was in Gerry's position, I think I would have slipped the ball to the back post because it was a guaranteed goal. Perhaps, with time already up, it's just as well our 'Man of the Match' had possession then.

There was still time for me to play a small part in making sure of the win and so I was back tormenting their goalkeeper Peter Burke again. The ball rebounded out of the net from Gerry's strike and as Burke went to grab it for a quick kickout, I booted it into the crowd. Bad sportsmanship?

Maybe, but it killed any hope Burke had of a quick kickout.

THE CELEBRATIONS STARTED with a full-scale pitch invasion at the full-time whistle and continued across the county and beyond for the rest of the week. The weather, a home game, a last-gasp Connacht final win over Mayo… not even Steven Spielberg could have written a better script!

That week, we visited a few of the county town's finest establishments with our new friend JJ Nestor in tow. It was a great feeling, but if I'm honest, I have always struggled to enjoy post-match celebrations like that. There is little comfort for the players because everywhere is packed and we're usually mentally and physically drained.

The supporters are fantastic, but it can be difficult to relax and enjoy the moment in those situations. The day after a final was probably more enjoyable for us because we got to sit down with our teammates and have the craic. Moments like that are why you train and put the effort in each year.

TOBY GAVE US the week off after the Connacht final, which, in hindsight, was probably the worst thing he could have done with that team! Some players used it as an excuse to go on the mother of all sessions, and by that stage of my development, I was certainly no different.

Midway through the week, a gang of us were out enjoying a few quiet pints with Francie Grehan in Ballyforan, when one of the lads stuck his head in the door and asked if any of us would be interested in a trip to Cork.

Being young and hell-bent on knocking as much craic out of the week as I could, there was only one response to such an invitation.

'Cork? Yeah… why not!'

It was already late in the evening but off the Roscommon rebels went on the road to Cork! Our driver hadn't been drinking but myself and a friend of mine called Mike Costello had had a few before setting off. In fact, we were so well oiled that we didn't realise how long the drive would be. Our teammate never told us why he was heading down that way and we never really asked. I think he just wanted a change of scenery.

Our patience was wearing thin by the time we got to Cork, and then it completely ran out when he told us we were actually heading for Skibbereen! He wasn't too long out there enjoying his change of scenery before we convinced him to take us home.

I went straight to bed as soon as I got back to Kiltoom the following morning, before it was time to head up to Dublin for a few more nights on the beer. It was mad stuff, but most of us were young enough at that stage to recover.

Let me tell you though, if I thought the nights out were wild that week in Roscommon, Dublin was on another level. We spent four nights in-a-row in Copper Face Jack's that week and yet we still haven't received our Gold Membership cards!

WE MIGHT HAVE played hard, but we made sure we worked hard too. By the end of our mad week off, we were back training like dogs in Ballyforan while we waited to hear who our opponents would be in the All-Ireland quarter-final.

It might seem strange, but there was a feeling of deflation when Galway's name came out of the hat again that year. That's usually the case when you're drawn against a team you've already played – there was also a worry that it might be asking a bit much to beat that Galway team twice in the same year.

There was also a certain amount of fear due to the momentum Galway had built up on their run through the qualifiers. While we went on the beer after the Connacht final, Galway had been playing game after game with no time for wild nights out. They had been lucky at times, particularly when they pipped Armagh by a single point in round two, but they were getting tough games, while we had only played Mayo in the previous few weeks.

To make things worse, the game was scheduled to be played in Castlebar rather than at Croke Park, which was a disappointment. Very few of us had the opportunity to tog out at Croker before so we felt we were missing out on the experience.

Our record in Castlebar hardly inspired a lot of confidence either.

All our worst fears were realised in MacHale Park that day. We simply didn't show up and Galway turned the tables on us. They bottled us up and restricted us to a goal and five points. It was pathetic really. They ran out comfortable six-point winners in the end and would go on to secure their ninth All-Ireland title that year, becoming the first side to come through the qualifiers and lift the Sam Maguire.

The disappointing end to our championship campaign meant a return to club action with St Brigid's – so my shoulder surgery would have to wait until November at the earliest. Over the next few months, an injured shoulder would turn out to be the least of my worries, however.

WE HAVE SADLY lost two teammates since Gerry Lohan's heroics on that beautiful July day at Dr Hyde Park.

Ger Michael Grogan had just been introduced to the panel in 2001 and came on at the end of our All-Ireland quarter-final against Galway. He was some athlete, about 6' 4" of lean muscle. He looked to have a bright future in midfield for both the county and his club Roscommon Gaels. He came from good Roscommon stock and his father Christy Snr had played in the All-Ireland final of 1962, while his brother Chris was a solid goalkeeper too. Gerard was only 23 when he sadly lost his life in a road traffic accident in March 2002.

I'll never forget getting the phone call from Francie Grehan that morning. I was in my room when he called to tell me what had happened. I couldn't get my head around it. It just didn't seem real.

The whole panel was stunned by the news and our National League game against Galway was called off as everyone tried to absorb it. I remember calling up to his family's house for his funeral – seeing his weights bench in one of the rooms and this sadness just fell over me. It wasn't just me either, there seemed to be a black cloud hanging over the whole town for a long while afterwards.

THE TALENTED CONOR Connelly also died in the month of March. Conor passed away suddenly while out running near his home in 2020. He was only 44. With Covid-19 restrictions, we couldn't attend his funeral but there were tributes to him all over Roscommon, Creggs and further afield as people hung flags out in his memory.

I had played with Conor for a few years and was even at his wedding at the Radisson Hotel in Athlone. He was always great craic on a night out and he and his wife Claire came to our wedding in the Sheraton in 2010 too. We were the last ones to leave the residents' bar that night!

He was a qualified solicitor and lived with Claire and their three kids in Ballycumber in Offaly, where he was highly thought of. Conor was the sort of fella who'd be thought highly of anywhere he went though.

Unlike Ger, he wasn't built like a unit, but he was an athlete and one of the strongest men I've ever met. I'll never forget the time a few of us were standing outside Flannery's Pub in Dublin in the middle of a session. Conor and Nigel Dineen would sometimes argue over which one of them was stronger.

Not that it really mattered because they were both animals! Conor was in fine form that night though and decided the time was right to put it up to Nigel.

'Take a walk back there, Dineen… and see if you can knock me over,' he said, laughing to himself.

There was plenty of drink taken at this stage, and Dineen was only too happy to oblige. He took a couple of steps back and hit Conor with a fierce shoulder. They rest of us winced, but Conor barely budged. He just walked off, still laughing.

That was the end of that argument.

No more than myself, he could be stubborn, but he was always a gentleman. He was also a great man for advice ahead of disciplinary hearings! He even helped us draft our apology letters following the infamous 'Naked Pool' incident the year after our Connacht championship win.

He was a very impressive guy, but he was also a terrific footballer and athlete too. Conor scored our first point at the Hyde against Mayo in 2001. I felt he could have slipped me in for a goal at the time but there you go, pure stubborn!

MY SHOULDER INJURY at the end of 2001 couldn't have come at a worse time. I had just started working for a phone company in Athlone and the new boss wasn't too happy when I asked for time off so I could go in for surgery. He basically told me that it was up to me but that my position wouldn't be there when I got back.

The job had come along at a time when I was badly in need of work too. I had joined the ESB straight out of school and worked there for almost four years. But the work became unbearable. With the ESB you are put with a crew of other lads and you work with the same lads every day.

You'll find this hard to believe, but I fell out with one or two of the lads in my gang and requested a transfer. When that request was turned down, I decided it was time to move on and I handed in my notice.

Thankfully, I had found a bit of work stocking coffee machines for Emmett Durney, who would go on to manage the Roscommon minors. I had worked with Emmet before, picking carrots during the summer when I was still in school. The coffee machines were a little bit easier on the back though, thank God. Emmett was a sound fella to work for and while it was never going to be long-term, I was grateful for the job at the time.

I moved on to the phone shop and I was only there a couple of months when the time came to repair the shoulder. It was just a few weeks before Christmas and a more sensible fella probably would have waited it out, but I just wanted to be fit for Roscommon in 2002. Short-sighted? Maybe.

But nothing mattered more to me than football back then.

The surgery took place at the Blackrock Clinic and it went well. Afterwards, I stayed with friends in Dublin for a few days to recuperate. I was sleeping on the couch downstairs when I got up to use the toilet one night.

As I was making my way back down to the living room, I missed one of the stairs and tumbled all the way to the front door. There was no alcohol involved, I swear! It was just one of those things.

And I nearly put my foot through the door with the pain.

Fortunately, the shoulder was still intact, but I had torn the stitches and would need to be patched up. Other than that, and a bruised ego, I was fine.

THAT EGO OF mine would take even more of a battering in the New Year as I tried to work my way back to fitness. It's a lonely existence when you're out of the loop and training by yourself. Normally, when life got tough off the pitch, I had football to fall back on, but in early 2002 I was unemployed and facing a long spell on the sidelines. It wasn't good for a young fella's head.

I've no problem admitting now that I was in danger of going under in the early part of that year. I was feeling sorry for myself and just really fed up with everything.

That's the part of amateur or even professional sport that the supporters and pundits don't get to see. I had gone from the high of winning a Connacht title at the Hyde to the lows of unemployment and struggling to keep my head straight in the space of just a few short months.

THERE WERE OTHER complications too, both on and off the field. My mother and father had officially separated just a few weeks after the Connacht final the previous year. That was something that had played on mind, but I wasn't ready to speak about it at the time. Without football, I didn't have a release valve and so I just sat and stewed on everything.

As if all that wasn't bad enough, I had also fallen out with officials at St Brigid's around that time too. I've no doubt that it was all connected in some way, but at the time, I was just too angry to analyse these problems in any meaningful way.

My issues with St Brigid's had started after I returned to the club following our defeat to Galway in the All-Ireland quarter-finals. Myself and two other lads David O'Connor (AKA Jimmy Nail) and Ger Tiernan, had booked a two-week holiday in The Canaries. The problem was that our championship semi-final against Roscommon Gaels had gone to a replay and that clashed with our holiday dates.

The Gaels were the dominant force in Roscommon by then, but confidence was building in Kiltoom after the drawn game. It had been a long year though and with the shoulder the way it was, I was looking forward to being able to lounge by the pool with a few beers.

We quickly discovered that the only way to keep everyone happy was if we came back for the match midway through the holiday and then flew back to The Canaries afterwards. So, we agreed to return on the Thursday, play the match at the weekend and be back by the pool on Tuesday at the latest.

Joe Mulvihill, my old Athlone Community College coach, was over us at this point and he worked a deal with two committee members to get us back for the match. The club kindly agreed to pay for our flights back and to arrange a weekend away for us when the championship came to an end. It seemed fair to everyone. We were having a blast in The Canaries and found it difficult to return to the thick of championship football, but a deal's a deal and it is part of life as a senior player.

You get used to missing out on big events such as family weddings and birthdays... even my own wedding would be scheduled for the 'off season'. A flight home from The Canaries is a minor inconvenience compared to some of the things you have to do!

To be fair, we should have won the first game, but John McHale had levelled things up late on with a free. I had played well and scored a goal and four points, but it just wasn't enough, and we had to go at it again when we should have been on the beach.

BACK WITH A slight tan, I did well in the replay too and ended up with another high total, which just goes to show that a few nights on the beer did me no harm.

I was guilty though of missing a late free to take the game to another replay the following weekend. Maybe somewhere in my subconscious I just wanted to stay by the pool! Whatever the reason, the ball hit the post and the referee blew full-time on our championship.

I drowned my sorrows at Jimmy Nail's house that night before we made our way to Dublin Airport the following day to restart our holiday.

And what a restart it was too!

We bumped into the former Boyzone star Ronan Keating while waiting for our flight at one of the airport bars. *Life is a Rollercoaster* had just been released the year before and so, already in good spirits, we decided it was an ideal opportunity to serenade Mr Chart Topper. Sadly, he didn't appreciate our performance at all and told us to 'f**k off'.

When we got back from our stop-start holiday I approached the two committee members from before to see about arranging the weekend away they had promised us. They were quite abrupt and quickly informed me that nothing had been agreed with the club at board level. There would be no weekend away at the Galway Bay Hotel… or anywhere else.

Nothing agreed? That came as a surprise to me.

One of the reasons we had agreed to give up five days of our holiday was because the club had promised to make it up to us. I felt stung. I couldn't believe they had gone back on their word like that. It was a painful reminder of the time Athlone Town had refused to pay for my knee surgery.

The anger and hurt festered in me over the following weeks and I came to the decision that I was finished putting my heart and soul into representing the club. I couldn't be around some of the officials anymore, so there was no other option but to move on.

« CHAPTER 8 »

I WOULD FACE some of the toughest moments of my life during those months from the end of 2001 to the middle of '02. But, once again, Gaelic football would provide me with a means of escape and a way of restoring my pride.

The early part of the year though was especially difficult as I continued my recovery. There was little football played and that made it difficult to maintain my fitness levels.

I was itching to return to any sort of action.

I was eased back into the team during the league matches that year. Roscommon had a decent campaign and finished top of Division 1A, beating Dublin at Parnell Park in the process. The late Eugene McGee even dubbed us 'The new pin-up boys of football' after that performance. We only lost one game during the league phase and that was to a Tyrone team which was headed for greatness.

We qualified for the semi-finals comfortably, but our results didn't tell the whole story. While we were getting the plaudits for our attacking play, there were serious question marks over our defence. We had somehow managed to top the division with a points difference of minus two.

It was an outrageous statistic. We had scored nine goals and 90 points in seven games but had shipped nine goals and 92 points.

Despite the defensive concerns, the hype was beginning to build around us and some supporters bought into it. We never seem to learn to manage our expectations.

SOME OF THE supporters I spoke to were in denial, telling me that we'd sort out our defensive troubles before the championship and then we'd be formidable.

'No need to panic... Toby will tighten us up!'

That was easier said than done.

While we were glowing off the positive headlines in the local and national media, counties like Tyrone, Galway and Dublin were using the league campaign as preparation for bigger games. The Galway side we had drawn with in the spring would be a completely different animal come the summer. It felt like we were kidding ourselves.

My fears were confirmed in the league semi-final against Cavan. We were brought back down to earth with a bang as they put five goals past us in Mullingar. The hype and the headlines weren't long vanishing with the All-Ireland champions on the horizon.

TO GET US back on track for our Connacht championship opener against Galway, John Tobin arranged to take us up to Donegal for a challenge match.

What could go wrong?

We had a decent run out against Donegal and were sitting in the dressing-room chatting away when Toby arrived in.

'Right lads, still plenty to work on next week but tonight we're going to enjoy ourselves.'

Great! A few pints to let off some steam before the big one.

Toby wasn't finished.

'We're not heading back to Roscommon tonight. We're going up to Derry!'

Lads were in the middle of getting changed to head home. Nobody seemed prepared for a night out anywhere, never mind cross-border.

'What are we going to Derry for?'

'Just for a few pints... we've a hotel booked.'

Toby or the county board must have got a great deal with the hotel because it made absolutely no sense otherwise.

MOST OF THE lads had travelled up in their Roscommon gear and I don't think anyone had brought a spare change of clothes. We didn't even have pounds sterling for pints. I had assumed we were going up to play our match against Donegal and then turning around and heading for home. Pints in Derry? No chance.

Pints were pints though, so we piled onto the bus and hit the road! I remember arriving at the hotel and a few of us had to go around scrounging money so that we weren't left sipping the free water in our rooms.

We hit the town and it didn't take long for everyone to be enjoying themselves. The lads were in good spirits but there was certainly no messing or anybody falling over drunk or causing a scene. A tame night out if you ask me!

A GROUP OF us arrived back at the hotel after closing time. The place looked completely deserted apart from a barman, so we made our way to the games room which was in a snug hidden away from the main bar. It was around two o'clock in the morning at this stage, so we decided to have a game or two of pool... then head to bed.

Everyone was in fine form at this stage so before the balls were racked, I suggested playing 'shirts and skins' for a laugh. The lads jumped on this of course and decided we'd use a coin toss to determine who would have to strip off.

In what was one of the biggest backfires in the history of Roscommon GAA, I lost the toss and myself and my doubles partner were forced to strip. If only I could have known the impact a simple flip of a coin could have...

Our opponents that night fancied themselves as pool sharks at the time, and we thought it would be great if they were beaten by two lads in the nip! We managed to win the game, not that anyone has ever really been interested in that part of the night!

At one point, I was standing there, stark naked, thinking... *If anyone could see us now!*

There were four of us involved in the game of pool, while one of the other lads had fallen in under the table and was getting kicked every time he tried to get back up.

OK WE MIGHT have been a bit rowdy and laddish, but it was all just a bit of harmless fun and we all went to bed that night and thought nothing more of it.

What we didn't know at the time was that 'Big Brother' was watching us. The pool room had a high ceiling and right up in the far corner of the room there was a CCTV camera. It was almost impossible to detect, especially if you've been out on the beer all evening!

We knew we were in trouble the next morning before breakfast.

It turned out that someone got hold of the tape from that camera and brought it straight to the *Sunday People* newspaper. We then got word that the paper was planning to publish the story in that weekend's edition.

It was the worst case of 'beer fear' you could ever wake up with.

I was sitting in a friend's house when it came out. It wouldn't have been a widely read paper in the south, but word got out that we were about to make our page three debuts, resulting in record sales in the Republic that weekend!

For as long as I live, I will never forget my very own little newspaper review that Sunday morning. One of my mates arrived in with the paper at eleven o'clock as I was sipping on a pint of Guinness to settle the nerves. From pioneer to exhibitionist in the space of four short years as a Roscommon footballer!

He was leafing through the paper at this stage… eyes widening.

'Jaysus, Frankie… ya know it's actually not that bad.'

'Let me see!' I said, grabbing it off him.

It was right across the front page.

'You don't think this is bad? It's alright for you… you're not on show… stark naked!'

I took a bigger mouthful and a deep breath.

Then I turned to the next two pages to see a big splash of us in all our glory. 'AHHH… F***K!'

To make matters worse, they had the Nestor Cup covering my bits. Talk about rubbing it in.

I HAVE LEARNED to put that incident in Derry into some perspective. It was my idea to play 'shirts and skins' that night and I hold my hand up and accept the part I played. I apologised for it at the time and meant it. The fallout was over the top though in my opinion and it had a big impact on me and other fellas on that team.

To be fair, that sort of messing went on and probably still goes on in every club and county as well as in every other code too. I know for a fact that there have been worse incidents involving other counties which never managed to make the papers. It always amazed me how the stories involving Roscommon would somehow find their way into the public domain. *What were we doing wrong?*

The important thing to remember is that it was all just a bit of fun. No-one was hurt. When a group of lads get together and there are pints involved, then there are pranks played and some childish messing does go on.

For example, I remember another incident a couple of years after that in Kiltoom of all places.

IT WAS AFTER a match with St Brigid's and we were sitting in a little snug in one of the local pubs. There must have been 30 of us or so, crammed in there having a singsong. Nothing out of the ordinary except for the fact that we were all stark naked!

I don't know what the fascination is or was with getting our clothes off, but it was great craic all the same. Why did we do it? There was no real reason apart from a bit of devilment. There was no bullshit or trouble... obviously we were just extremely comfortable with each other! I had also learned by this stage to check for CCTV cameras so there was little fear of anything appearing in the *Roscommon Champion*.

Two of the lads found Hi-Viz jackets in the pub that day, the kind county council workers wear. They thought it would be hilarious to go out onto the road outside and stage a checkpoint.

They were well on it and we were in stitches as we watched them pulling cars in, asking to see drivers' licences and tax discs, wearing nothing but the Hi-Viz jackets. Thankfully, it wasn't a busy road and the few drivers who were stopped took it in good spirits. Imagine pulling that prank these days with camera phones and social media!

THE NEWSPAPER IMAGES of the 'Naked Pool' episode were embarrassing enough but the inaccurate story which was published alongside them made things even worse for us. It was said that we had wrecked the hotel, caused damage to our rooms and really pissed off the other guests. None of that was true.

We were near the residents' bar and there wasn't another soul in or near the pool room that night and nobody could have seen us from the main bar either. There was one barman in the main bar but none of us went out anywhere near him once the game started.

It was all just a bit of craic amongst ourselves. Was it childish? Yes, it probably was but we weren't being a nuisance to anyone else. Afterwards, I think we mostly felt stupid for not spotting the CCTV. If we had seen it then, obviously we would have thought twice about getting our kit off.

Neither my parents, or my brothers and sister, passed any comment when the story came out, nor did my poor girlfriend at the time. They didn't need a Sunday newspaper to tell them we were eejits, I suppose! People in general realised very quickly that there was no-one hurt or harmed in the making of the video, however.

I have learned to laugh about it now, but one thing about the incident has always stuck with me and that was the lack of protection or support we received from the county board. I still feel they hung us out to dry after the incident and didn't do enough to prevent the story from being published.

We were hurt at the time because we were aware of other incidents involving the 'bigger' counties where their county boards had managed to keep things quiet. I could never get my head around the fact that the Roscommon County Board couldn't or wouldn't do the same for us.

Every team was at the same craic in those days.

They all enjoyed pints after a game and a bit of messing. It was never anything serious anyway but at least they could rely on the support of their own officials if things did ever get out of hand.

ROSCOMMON GAA'S HANDLING of the Derry incident just added to the belief I had that there was someone within the camp undermining us, willing certain players to fail. Maybe it was a Roscommon official who enjoyed being in the middle of the pub gossip, or a player who was struggling to break into the team.

I haven't a clue, but I do believe that our antics were a welcome distraction at times for the county board, who came under regular scrutiny for their own missteps.

During that era everything we did seemed to become public knowledge. It wasn't just in the national media either, certain members of the local press enjoyed having their say too.

There were times when we would be out enjoying ourselves and players from other counties were with us. They never seemed to be questioned about their discipline though. Maybe we were all paranoid in Roscommon, but it irritated us because we trained as hard as everyone else. I can guarantee that any time I set foot on a football pitch I worked as hard as I physically could.

If we went drinking after a championship game and had training on the Tuesday, the leaders in that team would always make damn sure they were out in front for any running or drills. We played hard, but by God did we work hard.

I GREW UP quickly in 2002. I was pretty much dealing with the fallout by myself at the time, which was just the way it was back then. If something like that happened now you would have every sports psychologist in Ireland contacting a player offering their services, which is not a bad thing.

I was forced to suffer in silence at the time though, which I see now wasn't the right way to handle things. I didn't have to suffer alone. There were plenty of well-meaning people trying to help me, but I was just too pig-headed to let them in.

Looking back, I was probably going through a bit of depression. It would be a few years before I could speak about it properly, however, and even then, it would take a breakdown to bring it out into the open.

In that moment, football was still the best form of escape and I was slowly returning to full match fitness after my shoulder injury and my ill-fated pool debut when we played Galway in the Connacht championship quarter-final at the Hyde that May.

I wasn't named in the starting 15 because I wasn't quite up to speed, but I came on and took a penalty. It was against Alan Keane, the giant goalkeeper from Killererin, who stood at 6' 5" and seemed to take up most of Dr Hyde Park.

I usually went top right with my penalties, knowing that if the ball was struck well no goalkeeper would be able to get near it. Not even a man mountain like Alan!

I had perfected my routine even down to the number of steps in my run up. I placed the ball, ignoring the jeers of the Galway supporters behind the goal, who were shouting things like 'Here's Steve Davies!' and 'Go on Ronnie!' in honour of my pool exploits.

I thought… *I'll show ye bastards!* And I stepped back and ran forward to smash the ball into the top corner. Except this time there was too much power behind the shot and the ball skimmed the crossbar and went over, much to the delight of my new fans in maroon and white.

I was later told that the ball had come back off the scoreboard, hitting my sister Kara's then boyfriend in the back of the head, causing him to lose some teeth! In fairness to him, he wasn't the only Roscommon man lacking bite at the Hyde that day and we limped out of the Connacht championship on the end of a 10-point hiding.

As if our defeat to Galway wasn't bad enough, Mayo then sent us crashing out of the championship in the second round of the qualifiers. It was a nightmare year, and we were looking forward to putting it behind us, but we weren't out of the woods just yet.

That July we were summoned to a meeting in the old Royal Hotel in Roscommon town by the county board. I wasn't at the meeting, but I was told about it afterwards.

In a move that was described as… *Dramatic, extreme and unprecedented* in the national media, the county team was disbanded just one year on from winning the Connacht title.

The chairman listed off several rumours of indiscipline that were circulating around the county at the time. Those present were asked to swear that they weren't involved in any of them.

It's something that would be unheard of today.

Roscommon was officially an embarrassment from head to toe.

PART FOUR

Outside of the Right

« CHAPTER 9 »

I WAS ALREADY getting tired of the controversy that seemed to go hand in hand with being a Roscommon footballer. I was certainly sick of all the sniggering and slagging that went on after the whole 'Naked Pool' episode.

At that stage, I was out on the road working for Tullamore Foods and everyone I came across seemed to have heard all about my escapades. I was more famous as a pool player than I was as a county footballer!

I covered Kildare, Laois, Offaly and Westmeath as part of my weekly routine, which included regular visits to everything from big supermarkets to smaller village shops. I quickly got the feeling that people struggled to take me seriously, and in some places, the slagging would start as soon as I arrived at the shop.

I remember walking into a shop one morning in Portlaoise and a fella I had never laid eyes on before shouted, 'Here he comes now… the naked pool player!'

The slagging did affect me, but I still refused to deal with it, preferring to shut it out or avoid it altogether. It was in that headspace that I decided I would be better off leaving the country for a while. I was sure that it would all blow over after a few weeks and things would go back to normal.

AS MUCH AS I wanted to head off though I couldn't just drop everything and go. After falling out with St Brigid's over our holiday debacle at the end of 2001, I had decided to make a clean break and sign with Ballymahon in Longford.

The transfer had come about because my uncle Dessie was involved with the management set-up there and I could hear how passionate he was about the club every time he spoke.

I've always had great respect for Des, who's not only a great football man but also someone who has given me sound advice throughout my career. When he heard what happened at Brigid's it didn't take him long to make his pitch.

'You need to be playing football, Frankie. Ya can't be walking away at your age. 'Why not come and train with us?

'The lads are sound.'

The idea of a fresh start was simply too good to turn down and Ballymahon had a good set-up with Christy Mannion as manager and great club men like the chairman Mick Cooney and secretary Derek Fahy. Everything was in place, so I put in for a transfer and I went to play my football in Longford ahead of the 2002 season.

Despite falling out with some of the St Brigid's officials, I found it hard to leave Kiltoom at the end of 2001. But that didn't mean it wasn't the right thing to do at the time. They say a change is as good as a break and I think my two years with Ballymahon proved that.

Football in Longford was completely different to what I had experienced in Roscommon. There's always a target on your back when you're a county player, but when you're a county player playing in a different county it's even worse. I received no protection from the referees and that toughened me up and helped me to realise the importance of looking after myself on the pitch. Though I always had my suspicions that some referees enjoyed watching me getting roughed up a little too much!

To be honest, I probably didn't do much to endear myself to the officials either. There's one game in particular that sticks out in my mind.

We were playing in the championship against Mullinalaghta and we were winning well. The referee must have felt sorry for them or something because he gave them a rake of soft frees in the second-half. I had already been booked earlier in the game but when he awarded them another free towards the end, I lost my patience and grabbed hold of the ball.

'Give me that ball!' he barked at me.

With that I threw it up in the air and booted it out over the press box. It was about the sweetest contact I ever made with a football – I swear, the ball must have gone 70 yards!

'If you want it… then go get it!'

He couldn't get my second yellow card out fast enough.

It was clear during my time there that I would get nothing easy. The regular special treatment and the fact that I had to fight and defend my corner really did make a man out of me though. The same way that my off-field problems during that period would help me to mature as a person.

Overall, the move to Longford was a welcome relief to be honest because I think all the controversy would have been much harder to deal with if I had still been playing my club football in Roscommon.

Besides, after the way in which the two boys and myself had been treated by St Brigid's, I don't think I would have enjoyed my football in Roscommon that year anyway. A separation was best for all parties.

I HAVE ALWAYS felt that sport can have a powerful impact on a person's mental well-being. That first year with Ballymahon was further proof of this. The club had never won the senior county title until we beat Clonguish at Pearse Park that year. We also won the league in 2002 so maybe I was the club's new lucky charm!

I had gone there with my mind made up to let my football do the talking and it wasn't long before I was enjoying myself again. There was a terrific buzz around the club in the build-up to the final and I could forget about everything else and just be part of that. I scored a goal and eight points against Clonguish in that game to continue my great record in county finals. The team was at the right age as well and we believed we could go on and do some damage in Leinster that year.

We were still confident even when drawn against the reigning Leinster champions Rathnew in the semi-final. If we wanted to do the unthinkable and bring home a Leinster title, then we knew we'd have to beat the best teams.

I still have vivid memories or even nightmares of that semi-final. There was a torrential downpour all morning. I've still no idea how the game got the go-ahead. Those were some of the most difficult conditions I have ever played football in and it didn't help that we were faced with a tough Rathnew side.

Maybe my head was already on holiday at that stage, but my season certainly fell apart. I just couldn't get it together. At times it felt as though I was chasing shadows in boots full of lead. It was right up there with one of my worst days on a football pitch. I was forcing shots that were never on just to spark some sort of revival, both for myself and the team.

I WAS BEING marked by Eamon White that day, and he did a good job of keeping me scoreless from play. That being said, my decision-making made his job a whole lot easier. I'd say he couldn't believe his luck!

It wasn't just me stinking the place out either. It was a dreadful match and Rathnew trudged out 0-8 to 0-6 winners even though we had kept them scoreless in the second-half. We only managed two points after the interval, and I think it went down as a plucky performance by the Ballymahon underdogs against the big guns from Wicklow. It should have been so much more.

That game was such a disappointment for the club and for me personally. I had a brilliant year in Longford and was in great form in the run-up to it. As the go-to guy when it came to scores, I felt I had let my teammates and the club down when it mattered most. If we had managed to overturn Rathnew in that game, things could have been quite different, and we could have had a really good run in Leinster that year. It was a missed opportunity.

I WAS GOING out with a girl in Dublin at that time, who had been born in Australia and so when the club season came to an end, we decided to head Down Under together for a few weeks. My head was fried, and I was falling out of love with football, so the time was right to get away and press the reset button.

Australia turned out to be the perfect escape because nobody cared about naked pool or Roscommon football in general out there. We spent about three months travelling around Brisbane and the Gold Coast, and forgot about everything for a while.

By the time we got home, the relationship may have been fizzling out, but at least I was back in love with Gaelic football again! I was hungry to get back playing at the top level and prove all the doubters of the previous year wrong.

« CHAPTER 10 »

FOLLOWING THE DISBANDMENT of the team in 2002, the former Dublin footballer and manager Tommy Carr took charge of Roscommon ahead of the following season. Tommy would be in charge for nearly three years until 2005, before 'player power' ousted him – and while our time together started well in that beautiful summer of 2003, I had walked away from the panel by the end of his reign.

WE GOT OFF to a good start though, and after Tommy accepted the job in 2003 he invited me to meet with him at a restaurant in Kinnegad. I agreed and we ended up chatting for almost two hours about football and life in general. The meeting was clearly aimed at testing the waters following the events of the previous year.

I'm sure Tommy met with some of the other lads too to make sure we were all fully committed to the cause. He had nothing to worry about in that regard though because we always were.

I was impressed that he had made the effort and I explained to him that I wasn't long home from Australia. I was honest with him and told him straight out that I had needed to get away for a while to clear my head. I also gave him assurances that I was hungry to come back and put the record straight.

There were plenty of critics waiting to be silenced, I told him.

In short, I wanted to forget all about 2002 and put my stamp on 2003 and prove what I believed, that I was one of the best forwards in the country. I can honestly say that sitting in Kinnegad that day, I was excited about a new start with a new manager, who seemed to be taking an interest in his players on a human level.

TOMMY WAS VERY much hands on when it came to training. He had only retired a few years earlier and he was still fit enough to get involved in the sessions himself. He did some of the running with us and wasn't afraid to step in during training games if we needed to make up the numbers.

We may not have won anything under Tommy, but we played some excellent football in both league and championship, and gave our supporters a few memorable days out in the process. Tommy's first year in charge was his best and we reached the All-Ireland quarter-finals, where we gave a decent account of ourselves against a good Kerry team at Croke Park.

From a personal point of view, while I'll always maintain that I played the best football of my career for St Brigid's, I had some of my best days for Roscommon while playing for Tommy. We started the year well with a narrow one-point win over Tyrone at Dr Hyde Park in the league. Mickey Harte's boys were the coming team, so it was a great boost for us to see them off, even if it was in the league.

Our form after that though was patchy and in the very next game we were obliterated by Kerry in Tralee. We ended up on the end of a 2-11 to 0-4 hiding, which was a real dose of reality after the Tyrone win.

We beat Cork in the next game at the Hyde which gave us some hope of staying in Division One. It was a really competitive league that year. The two Ulster sides Tyrone and Armagh would finish first and second respectively, but there was only a gap of four points between Tyrone and ourselves in the relegation zone. Every team, apart from Tyrone, lost at least three games during that campaign.

We were inconsistent throughout, beaten well by Armagh, before hammering Galway and then suffering a three-point defeat against Dublin at the Hyde. I kicked 10 points against the Dubs, and Stephen Cluxton made two brilliant saves from me. I got on well with Stephen – we trained together back in the day. He is an outstanding role model. We still could have avoided relegation by beating Donegal on the last day, but they managed to beat us by a goal to send us down.

THERE WAS NO respite for us that year or even an easy championship draw to help get us back on track. It would be Galway in the quarter-finals but we hoped that our league campaign would stand to us going into that game in Salthill.

Tommy had made the decision to take us to La Manga in Spain for a week-long training camp prior to the Galway game. La Manga was where the English football teams used to go ahead of major international tournaments. I think Paul Gascoigne even trashed Glenn Hoddle's hotel room a couple of years before we were there. Tommy Carr got away lightly so!

THE HEAT WAS unbearable in Spain. To avoid the hottest parts of the day, we trained at seven o'clock each morning and then again at five or six o'clock in the evening when it started to cool down. It was pure torture.

It took a while for us to see the benefits of those gruelling workouts and soon after arriving home, we were hammered by Kildare in a challenge game.

In truth, we were absolutely drained by our trip to La Manga. We went at the wrong time; it was something we should have done earlier in the year. Nowadays, there's more science behind fitness work, and strength and conditioning are built up over a couple of years rather than being crammed into a week or two.

La Manga left us flat and as a result, we just never got going against Galway. They took full advantage and beat us by four points. We were cursing it then, but our hard work in the Spanish heat would stand to us as the year went on.

OUR DEFEAT TO Galway came despite our captain and goalkeeper Shane Curran's best efforts to unsettle the opposition. We found out after the match that Cake had smeared one pair of gloves in Vaseline before giving Galway 'keeper Alan Keane a hearty handshake. Keane quickly realised what had happened though and managed to change his gloves before the throw in.

Cake was only getting started.

We were trailing by six at half-time when he arrived into the dressing-room and started telling us how much the game meant to the great people of Roscommon. He then reached into his kitbag and, holding up this plastic package, he said, 'Lads, this is Roscommon blood and we're going to have to spill Roscommon blood now to win this match!'

Then, to emphasise his point, he flung this bag of blood to the floor. But instead of bursting and spilling Roscommon blood all over us, it bounced and landed in the middle of the dressing-room, still fully sealed.

We looked at the bag... then looked at Cake, before looking back at the bag again. Every man in that dressing-room would have burst himself laughing if the situation wasn't so serious.

We found out later that Cake had gone to the doctor and asked him to take a pint of his blood so he could put it in that sealed bag. The idea was to take it out at half-time if we were trailing and inspire a second-half fightback.

Our bloodthirsty captain may not have led us to victory but something he said must have clicked with us because we went out and won that second-half against an excellent Galway team. God knows how far we could have gone that year if Cake's bag of blood had actually burst!

We got back on track with a nervy one-point win over Cork in the first round of the qualifiers on a day when Cork manager Larry Tompkins was nearly attacked by a pitch invader. There was a serious fall-out over that at the time and the Cork chairman Jim Forbes complained about the security arrangements in the national media. Forbes and Tompkins also claimed they hadn't been able to get into our dressing-room to congratulate us after the game. I've no idea what happened there but I do know the dressing-rooms at the Hyde could be chaotic at times.

Following all the controversy in the wake of the Cork game we were happy enough to be drawn against our neighbours Leitrim in Carrick-on-Shannon in round two.

We always fancied ourselves against Leitrim; it's probably been the same for most Roscommon teams in the past. Complacency crept in that day though and it took a late intervention from super-sub David O'Connor to save our bacon.

We were staring another embarrassing defeat in the face when I got a half-chance late on. It was just a case of getting the shot on target and making sure the ball stayed in play. I made decent contact, but it was pushed away by Garret Phelan, who had been a thorn in our side all afternoon. Nigel Dineen was following in though, and he kicked the ball into the ground before O'Connor arrived at the back post to smash it into the net.

Only for that goal, the whole year would have been a write-off and Tommy would have come under fierce pressure to step down. He admitted it himself after that we had used our 'Get out of Jail' card that day.

IN THE AFTERMATH of our winning goal, I became involved in a tangle with the Leitrim 'keeper Phelan and he was sent off. I used my favourite time-wasting tactic and kicked the ball away to delay his kickout, so he decided to kick me up the backside instead.

With nothing to lose, Leitrim somehow managed to sneak their sub-goalie Enda Lyons on for the last few seconds without taking anyone else off. It didn't matter in the end and we held on for a totally undeserved win. The pressure was off after that and we managed to get a run going as our fitness work began to really pay off.

It was widely accepted in most counties around this time that players socialised after a match. Not only did it help with bonding between players, but it also helped with the relationship between players and supporters too. We were amateur athletes and a central part of our communities after all. Sure, as long as you were able to give one hundred percent in training and matches, was there really any harm in it?

Well, Tommy Carr certainly thought so, and he pulled some of us in for a chat just before our third round qualifier against Offaly in Mullingar. A few of us had gone out the previous Sunday night and three of the lads had even been spotted in a well-known nightclub in Athlone town.

Tommy and his backroom team must have been under severe pressure to come down hard on any indiscipline after what happened in 2002.

As a result, Paul Noone, David O'Connor and John Nolan were dropped from the panel ahead of the Offaly game. It was particularly harsh on Noone because the Roscommon management had convinced him to cancel his plans to travel to the US earlier that summer. There was a feeling among some players that Carr's approach had been heavy-handed and once again it was in the national media that Roscommon had dropped players due to a breach of discipline.

WE TRAVELLED TO Cusack Park on a sunny Saturday in July knowing how lucky we were to still be in the championship but also determined to improve on our performance against Leitrim.

I was marking Offaly All Star Cathal Daly that day and it's fair to say that he had the better of me early on. The game was passing me by to be honest, and I could feel Tommy's eyes boring into me from the sideline. It felt like it was just a matter of time before I got the hook.

It has always fascinated me how the pattern of a game changes from one minute to the next. A sudden burst of confidence can completely transform a player's performance. That is exactly what happened that day in Mullingar.

The ball started coming my way, and I kept it nice and simple as I found my way into the game. I then started winning frees, which is a sure sign you're getting on top of your marker. All those hours of practice in the back garden begin to pay off when you're tapping over frees at Cusack Park.

The crowd cheers, your confidence grows and then you can take it up a level.

I WAS IN the groove now and I popped a sweet diagonal ball inside towards Gerry Lohan which was eventually gathered by Seamus O'Neill, and he was pulled down in the square. Gerry had his penalty saved but tapped in the rebound and we went in level at the break. 'Shak' O'Neill was doing well in getting forward from midfield and I felt like I was only getting started.

The second-half was just as tight, and the game looked to be heading for extra-time. I was buzzing at this stage, constantly looking for the ball and cleaning Daly out.

I think he knew it himself and I felt his head dropping in that second-half.

We were kicking into the end where the apartments were, and we won a lineball out near the dugouts. It must have been about 50 yards from goal but there was a nice breeze behind me as I prepared to take the kick.

Tommy Carr was shouting at me from the dugout.

'Put it dead… WHATEVER YOU DO!'

I just thought… *The cheek of you… I'm sending this over the bar!*

I pretended to ignore him. My confidence was sky-high at this stage and I knew the ball was going over the second it left the outside of my boot. A magical feeling.

I turned to the bench where Carr was standing.

'Is that dead enough for you, Tommy?'

I scored 12 points that day and was mobbed by Roscommon supporters at the end of extra-time. We were relieved more than anything that our summer had been extended and that we could look forward to more football.

Not surprisingly, Tommy's pre-match warnings fell on deaf ears and off we went in search of a session that evening!

WE GOT A good group of lads together and we all went out in Athlone. The Three Amigos… Johnny Dunning, the bould Paul Noone, and fun-time Frankie even ended up in Bozo's Nite Club together where the craic was ninety!

At the end of the night, we left the nightclub and were walking towards the pedestrian crossing on our way to the taxi rank. We noticed we were a man short and, sure enough, as we looked back in the direction of the nightclub, we could see a figure on all fours crawling across the pedestrian crossing.

It was the early hours of Sunday morning and there's a senior Roscommon footballer stopping traffic with his arse crack on display for half of Athlone to see!

All messing aside, it was crucial for us to go and blow off some steam after our hard-earned win in Mullingar. We were now ready to return to training to prepare for another do-or-die match against Kildare in round four.

Our Saturday night escapades would quickly become a distant memory as we huffed and puffed our way through a tough training session the following Tuesday night. Or so we thought.

The only break we got from the running that night came when Tommy called The Three Bozos in for a chat.

'Lads… ye were out drinking again?'

He must have paid off the Bozos doorman!

'Ah Tommy, that's just the way it is. We train hard and we play hard, but we enjoy a couple of pints afterwards.'

He wasn't letting it go.

'Not only were ye out drinking… one of ye was caught crawling like a f***in' child across a zebra crossing!'

There was no explaining that one away.

KILDARE, OUR OPPONENTS the following Saturday, were just off the back of a Leinster final defeat to Laois which was a bit of surprise. The backdoor system wasn't great for the team who lost at the provincial final stage and we believed they were a bit vulnerable. They were also carrying one or two injuries, which was another boost for us.

We had momentum going into that game and had started to enjoy our football. I came up against yet another All Star in the shape of Brian Lacey. Lacey was a real athlete, and a really strong player.

Our dual began in a similar way to the one I had with Cathal Daly in Mullingar. I was nowhere to be seen in the first 20 minutes or so. This time though, I remained confident that as the game went on, I would get more space, and sure enough I burst into life again in the second-half.

I was one of the most confident footballers in the country at that stage and I believe my performance that day in Portlaoise, in scoring 13 points, wiped the slate clean after what had happened the year before. It didn't matter who was marking me, I just wanted the ball.

JOHNNY DUNNING WENT to ground competing for possession about 30 metres out towards the end of extra-time. I followed in and clipped the ball into my arms. The angle was tight, but I was in the zone at that stage and kicked it over my left shoulder and it sailed over the bar.

Everything just clicked and I was feeding off the electric atmosphere.

We hadn't forgotten the beating Kildare had given us after we got home from La Manga either. Revenge was certainly a motivating factor for the clipping we experienced at Sean Mulryan's adoptive club Ballymore Eustace earlier that summer. Sean is still a very generous sponsor of Roscommon.

I still feel I should have scored 16 or 17 points that day, but the equalising point at the end of normal time was one of the best I have ever scored. Time was almost up and I'm sure there were Roscommon supporters urging me not to shoot.

It was just another one of those moments when I know it was going over. Kildare were completely deflated after that and we managed to finish the job in extra-time before our supporters streamed onto the pitch to celebrate. One of the great days.

OUR REWARD FOR beating Kildare was a Croke Park showdown with Kerry in the All-Ireland quarter-finals. The Kingdom had won the Munster championship earlier that summer and were rightly considered one of the favourites to lift Sam that year. It was the first time most of us had played at Croke Park and there was a real buzz as well as a few butterflies around the camp as we prepared for the big day.

We had a training session in Croke Park a few days before the game and the first thing I noticed was that the ball seemed to travel differently, especially when taking shots on goal at both ends of the ground. It might explain why I missed a couple of 'tap over' frees against Kerry!

I struggled to judge the breeze that day. It seemed to swirl in different directions around the big stadium. You nearly had to aim the ball five yards outside the post in some cases, depending on which way the wind was blowing at the time.

This isn't just some lame excuse, I promise.

In fact, a few years later, while I was on duty with St Brigid's, a Croke Park steward explained that the gap between the Hogan Stand and Hill 16 forced the wind to come in behind the goal at the Hill before swirling around the stadium and up behind the goal at the other end.

He said I wasn't the first to complain about it either. That's my excuse verified for those wides against Kerry anyway!

THE GAME ITSELF was great entertainment for the neutrals but it probably left both managers scratching their heads. It was a hot day in August and that Kerry team was full of runners, especially up around their half-forward line. Paul Noone was one of our most athletic players, but even he was finding it hard to get to grips with the Ó Sés and the O'Sullivans.

Kerry's pace just left us for dead and we also left far too much space for players like Colm 'Gooch' Cooper to exploit. Their whole team just seemed fitter and fresher than us and the conditions suited them. They were also well used to playing in front of 60,000 people.

Our nerves were obvious that day and at one stage we found ourselves trailing by about 11 points in the second-half. But as the game went on, we realised we had nothing to lose and that the Kerry back-line could be got at.

There was no real tactical masterplan or anything to get us back into the game. We just kept plugging away and finished with three goals, which raised a few eyebrows among the pundits at the time. Three goals and 10 points certainly wasn't a bad return and we probably deserved even more. Kerry were the better side overall, however, and deserved their place in the semi-finals.

IT WAS A tough way to end another year with Roscommon and I was disappointed that I couldn't add to my goal and three points. As well as some kickable frees, I missed a brilliant chance midway through the first-half, blazing over the bar when the goal was there for the taking.

It's no exaggeration to say that we could have scored six or seven goals. We weren't quite clinical enough when it mattered but we did ask serious questions of a Kerry team which went on to contest its eighth All-Ireland semi-final in nine years.

The most important thing for us was that our performances that summer went a long way to repairing Roscommon football's reputation on the national stage. We could be proud of that at least.

That summer still gets brought up in conversation even now. I've often been asked how I didn't manage to win an All Star that year considering my performances in the qualifiers and the quarter-final against Kerry. I can honestly say that I don't tend to lose too much sleep over it... or anything else really!

Most of the individual awards I have won are up in the attic anyway. I was named as a replacement All Star that year and of course it would have been nice to make it into the 15, but I didn't give it too much thought.

I went up to the All Star awards that year in Dublin. Most of the family were there and so too was a good friend of mine Mike Costello. We said we might as well enjoy ourselves while we waited to be called into the room where the awards were being presented.

We were really enjoying ourselves before the bell went to announce the start of the ceremony, and we started to make our way in. When we reached the doors leading into the other room one of the security men pulled me aside.

'Are those people with you?' he asked nodding behind me.

I turned around and there was Garvan and Mike carrying the table full of drink with them into the ceremony. I couldn't bring them anywhere!

ON A SERIOUS note, I think it's unbelievable that Roscommon has only ever had 11 All Stars but sometimes it does seem as though politics are involved in the decision-making process. Maybe the county board should have campaigned a little bit harder on my behalf in 2003.

There were three Laois players picked that year and I put that down to their legendary manager Mick O'Dwyer being more vocal ahead of the announcement than some of our own officials.

SIXTEEN YEARS LATER, I was down in Kerry for the October Bank Holiday with a couple of great friends of mine, John 'Patsy' O'Connor and Fergal Kelly.

Patsy kept at us to go for a pint in Páidí Ó Sé's bar in Ventry. Páidí had sadly passed away in 2012 but his son Páidí Jnr was still running the pub.

Myself and Fergal eventually agreed to head down for 'one or two'.

We were sitting up at the bar enjoying our pints when Patsy started chatting football with young Páidí. Our 'one or two' quickly became three and four, and some of the other punters were sharing their own stories about Páidí and Kerry football and asking me about my time with Roscommon.

Now, maybe they were blowing smoke up my backside, but the lads were telling me that nobody in the bar could believe how I hadn't won that All Star in 2003.

Even Páidí couldn't believe it, they said.

It could have been the few pints but there was certainly a lump in my throat after hearing that. I may have missed out on the official award but Páidí Ó Sé thought I was an All Star... and that was good enough for me.

« CHAPTER 11 »

AFTER AN IMPRESSIVE year in 2003, I was moved out closer to the '45' as Tommy tried to make the best use of my vision and passing ability. It never really worked out and I can remember feeling like an overworked tennis umpire in matches with the ball whizzing past me.

In fairness to Tommy, and my teammates, I wasn't doing what I was supposed to do and that resulted in the ball spending more time flying over my head than it did in my hand or on the end of my boot. I always wanted more of the ball so that I could deliver it down the throat of target men like Nigel Dineen; it just never arrived.

I could see exactly what Tommy was trying to do and I liked the idea of being responsible for pulling the strings in the Roscommon attack and bringing other players into the game.

It worked with St Brigid's when I was playing alongside the likes of Senan Kilbride, but it never really transferred properly to the county side.

When I think of playing effectively further out the field, players like Ciaran McDonald of Mayo come to mind. McDonald was brilliant at drifting into space and making himself available for a pass. His teammates were also on the same wavelength and they'd keep finding him with the ball. Mayo were set up to play with him as a playmaker, but we always struggled to operate in the same way in Roscommon.

IT IS FAIR to say that 2004 and '05 weren't great years for me personally, following the highs of 2003, when I was scoring for fun in the full-forward line.

Looking at the bigger picture, I don't believe the players gelled in the Roscommon panel perhaps as much as they should have. There was always a lot of chopping and changing going on, and I don't think I ever developed the same level of understanding with some of the lads that I would have had with teammates at club level.

My own role in the team was beginning to frustrate me too, because I had no idea where I would be playing from one match to the next. My head was wrecked with trying to figure out whether I'd be in the full-forward line or further out the pitch trying to dictate things. It made it impossible to visualise the game in the build-up.

If it were up to me, I would have been left in the full-forward line, where I had performed well in 2003. If it ain't broke, why fix it? I could genuinely see why Tommy wanted me further out the field, but I think the switch came too early in my career.

WE WON FIVE of our seven league games in 2004 but failed to gain promotion after losing to both Donegal and Offaly. We played some decent football at times but having to spend another year in Division 2A put a bit of a dampener on our championship preparations.

Sligo were the visitors to Dr Hyde Park in the Connacht quarter-finals that year. We put in a fairly average performance against them and were held to a draw. Things went from bad to worse for me in the replay at Markievicz Park. I was sent off for two yellow cards.

Ger Heneghan was substituted later in that game too, which meant that both our regular penalty takers were off the field when we were awarded a spot kick. Thank God our goalkeeper Shane Curran was there to convert it then!

Cake was in fine form that day and he also hit a brilliant point from a pressure free to put us ahead late on.

I'll never forget that moment. The lunatic put it over from the sideline and then took off towards his goal as if he'd won the lottery. He was jumping and roaring and punching the air all the way!

Cake's free shifted the momentum our way, but it just wasn't enough to win the game and Sligo snatched a late point to take it to extra-time.

Thankfully, we eventually managed to get ourselves together in the second period of extra-time to seal our place in the semi-finals. But the signs were ominous and even though our route to the final had looked straightforward, doubts were beginning to creep in.

THERE IS STILL no better game for getting a stuttering Roscommon team back on track than a championship game against Leitrim. At least on paper anyway. But if anyone ever thought our semi-final was a foregone conclusion, then they were in for a nasty surprise at Páirc Seán Mac Diarmada on June 20 that year.

We led for large chunks of the game, but we just didn't have the quality to finish them off. I scored six points and played okay, but they kept coming at us and Barry Prior grabbed a late equalising point to earn them a deserved replay.

The second game at Dr Hyde Park the following Saturday was a dreadful game, but we held Leitrim to five points and even though we only managed a goal and nine points ourselves, we ran out comfortable winners. We weren't exactly pulling up trees but at least nobody could claim we were being over-hyped ahead of the Connacht final!

Galway and Mayo were on the other side of the draw, and while we were struggling against the likes of Sligo and Leitrim, they were putting up outrageous scores ahead of their semi-final showdown in Castlebar.

Mayo hit 3-28 against New York, while Galway were even more ruthless in London and scored 8-14. Mayo were the comfortable winners in their semi-final and were heavy favourites for the final.

I COULD LIE and say that we were brimming with confidence going into that Connacht final, but I won't. Our worst nightmare came true that year in Castlebar when a cocky Mayo side hammered us by 10 points. Humiliation doesn't cut it. It does not get much worse for a Roscommon footballer than being slapped around by that crowd.

I came off at half-time after receiving a dead leg early in the first-half. As usual, some backs wait until the ball is turned over and everyone's focus is on the other end of the field and then drive a knee into the side of your thigh. Most of the time I could run it off but that day it slowed me down. Watching the second-half from the bench was an even more painful experience.

Worse was to come at the full-time whistle when Mayo manager John Maughan landed in our dressing-room to sympathise with us. A visit from the opposition is a normal occurrence, but that day we should have hung a sign on the door saying, 'House Private'. There were bodies everywhere, with some lads slouched against a wall and others standing motionless under the showers. There were boots and jerseys flung on the floor and it was eerily quiet apart from the sound of the running water.

It was into that heavy atmosphere that Maughan arrived.

I can still see him now, standing there with his hands on his hips as he spoke to us. He came across as pure arrogant.

For some reason, he went on and on about how good his own players had been as we just stared at the floor thinking of ways to kill him. Looking back, and knowing how proud a few of our lads were, he was lucky he wasn't run from our dressing-room in Castlebar that day. It might have saved Roscommon football some amount of hassle in the long run.

FOLLOWING THE EMBARRASSMENT of that Connacht final, we were drawn against Dublin in round four of the qualifiers. It would mean another chance to play in Croke Park and a bit of a glamour tie against the Dubs.

It wasn't a great Dublin team at the time either. They had good players but seemed to struggle to live up to the hype when it mattered. The Dubs didn't help themselves at times either and I seem to remember the following year they brought out a DVD about how they won the Leinster championship for the first time in three years. They were vulnerable that year though and we were confident we could turn them over.

Both sides played plenty of football that summer. We had five games in Connacht and the Dubs had entered the qualifiers all the way back in round one against London. They too had struggled to overcome Leitrim on their way to round four.

From a selfish point of view, I was really looking forward to another run out at Croke Park. The feeling was that we were due a good performance and were capable of taking a big scalp on our day. We had come up against the 'Boys in

Blue' in the league in previous years and we had a good record against them. We certainly didn't fear them anyway.

I had fully recovered from the dead leg I received against Mayo and I was raring to go for Croker. So, sure enough, Tommy announced that he was dropping me to the bench. No explanation given.

I was gutted but I also accepted his decision as part of the game. I refused to sulk and spent most of the game warming up on the sideline, trying to get his attention like an over-enthusiastic underage player. I knew I hadn't played well in the Connacht final but, then again, none of us had.

As usual though, it was the poor corner-forward who got it in the neck!

When I did come on for Johnny Dunning in the second-half, it was just too late to have any real impact on the game. I'll never forget the huge reception I got from the Roscommon supporters though. It was one of the loudest cheers of the day. Of course, Dublin had to go and ruin it by bringing on Dessie Farrell straight after!

The Dubs' hero of 1995 Jason Sherlock was still knocking around county football and he scored a lovely soccer-style goal as Dublin won by four points. Our championship was over for another year, but the Dubs crashed out in the quarter-finals against Kerry, who went on to beat Mayo in the final. There were very few tears shed in Roscommon about that, let me tell you!

I WAS FEELING a bit sorry for myself after the Dublin game. I felt hard done by and was convinced that had I played we would have had a better chance of winning that match. Maybe it was my ego doing the talking but I really felt the game was there for us if we had to courage to go and attack them.

Looking at the bigger picture, even at that early stage my county career had hit a bump in the road. It was mad considering I was only in my mid-twenties with my best football still ahead of me.

I decided not to dwell too much on the disappointment or to sit around feeling sorry for myself. It was better to shift my focus back to the club before hitting the ground running with Roscommon in the New Year.

By this stage, I had switched back to St Brigid's following two enjoyable years with Ballymahon. My first year in Longford had seen us win the league as well as an historic county title, but we couldn't repeat the feat in 2003, losing out in the final after a replay. Brigid's, on the other hand, still hadn't won a county title since 1997 – they had lost both finals in 2002 and '03.

I loved my two seasons with Ballymahon, but it was time to go back. I met the Brigid's chairman Peter McHugh at his house and got the transfer done. The prodigal son had returned just in time for an underwhelming year as we failed to reach the championship decider for the first time in three years, exiting at the quarter-final.

I decided then to take a short break at the end of 2004 before joining the gym at the Radisson Hotel in Athlone that winter. I was like a man possessed through November and December, and between the gym and the training pitch I must have logged hundreds of hours worth of workouts. I wanted to give myself the best chance possible of making an impression on Tommy Carr the following year.

Conditioning work was nothing new to me. I had always been fit but that winter I took it to another level completely. It was a lonely existence but there is something really satisfying about training hard when you know teammates and rivals are resting up. I kept telling myself I was ahead of everyone else and that helped with motivation on the cold and dark days.

The hard work paid off too and by the time we returned for our fitness tests at the start of 2005, I was leading the pack. The tests took place in the hall at the Hyde and the results showed that I was one of the fittest players on the panel. David Casey was usually head and shoulders above everyone else, but I wasn't too far behind him. It was clear to everyone that I meant business.

Back then it wasn't the norm for players to show up for pre-season training ready to go right out the gate. It was common for lads to go off for four or five months and enjoy their time off, and maybe put on a few pounds. I was glad then that I had taken the time to get myself into the best possible shape.

Sadly, my enthusiasm would prove to be very short-lived.

« CHAPTER 12 »

WE WERE DUE to play Clare in our first National League game of 2005 and by that stage I couldn't wait to get back out onto the pitch. You can imagine my disappointment then when Tommy named me as a substitute in the week of the game. Like most players, I didn't enjoy sitting on the bench. I wanted to be involved from the first minute to the last, and felt it was better to either start me or leave me out completely. I found it hard to sit and watch. I wanted to be in the thick of the action rather than just another onlooker.

Tommy eventually brought me on towards the end of the game, but as usual, there was hardly any time for me to make any significant impact.

To make matters worse, he slated me back in the dressing-room because I had coughed up possession. It's always going to be difficult bringing a player into the match late on and expecting him to win it for you. Sometimes it works and sometimes it doesn't.

On that day, the game ended in a draw.

Tommy's criticism stuck with me though. I didn't appreciate the way he tried to make an example of me, especially when other players had been on the pitch far longer. I can take criticism but at least give me a fair crack to prove you wrong.

We were due to face Carlow the following week, but Tommy clearly hadn't seen enough in the Clare game to change his mind about starting me in that one either. Once again, I was named as a substitute.

Whether he was trying to save me for later in the year or had just lost faith in me, I don't know. He had left me out of the panel at the start of the year, claiming I needed to recharge. But I had been recharging since the previous November.

Tommy's decision was nothing new. I had clearly fallen out of favour the year before when he dropped me for the qualifier against Dublin at Croke Park. I had taken that to heart and set out that winter to prove to him that I could play in whatever position he wanted to put me. I was fitter than I had been in years but sitting on the bench for Roscommon against the likes of Clare and Carlow didn't appeal to me. I'd had enough.

The St Brigid's dinner dance was the Friday night before the Carlow game. I had been at Roscommon training earlier in the evening – when the team was announced for the weekend. I was beside myself when I arrived at the Hodson Bay Hotel that night. I told some of the lads and the club chairman Peter McHugh that I was done with county football. Nobody took me seriously at the time- they told me to wait and see how I felt about it the following morning.

Nothing had changed when I woke up that Saturday morning and I still had no intention of travelling with the team for our league game against Liam Hayes' Carlow. I remember the phone rang a few times that Sunday. Francie Grehan and Nigel Dineen tried to reach me, but I just didn't have the heart to answer them.

I think it was one of the local reporters who asked Tommy where I was? He just mumbled something about me being sick, and unable to travel.

He was right about one thing... I was sick.

Sick and tired of being messed around with by the Roscommon set-up!

LOOK, I DON'T have to be told that I'm too stubborn sometimes. I know very well that I can be as thick as a ditch when I want to be. But I had committed myself to being at my absolute best for Roscommon and felt I was worthy of a place in that team. If it was part of Tommy's masterplan to leave me out to get more out of me later in the year, then he could have said something.

The Carlow game meant that I hadn't started for Roscommon since the Connacht final the year before and I struggled to see the justification for that because the team hadn't won any of those games.

It's fair to say that the drawn Carlow game was the beginning of the end for Tommy as Roscommon manager too. Those were games that our supporters expected us to be winning so to have just two points at that stage was bitterly disappointing. I know for a fact that a few of the more senior players were also annoyed about the situation and felt that I should have been playing. They had seen how desperate I was to get back into the team and how much being a Roscommon player meant to me.

They had asked me what was going on after the Carlow game and I told them the truth… I wasn't prepared to sit on the bench indefinitely after all the work I had put in. I think they understood my decision to walk away.

Like anything else there are good and bad moments in Gaelic football and performance levels can vary from game to game. With the benefit of hindsight, I can see now that I struggled at times in the years after 2002.

There were days when I was on a high, and other days when it felt like I was operating under a dark cloud. When Tommy dropped me, it was just the final straw.

I wasn't enjoying it anymore and just wanted out.

Tommy's reign as Roscommon manager came to an end after a defeat to Monaghan the following month. There had been a bit of unrest in the camp and after that league defeat in Clones it all came to a head. From what I could gather from being in contact with lads on the panel, the players had put pressure on the county board to act and the axe fell on Tommy.

On a lighter note, one of the lads later told me that a few of them had stopped off at a pub in Longford on the way home from that game in Clones. The nine o'clock news came on the television and the sports news had a report about the Monaghan game, as well as a league win for the Roscommon hurlers over Kildare.

One of the locals noticed the lads were wearing Roscommon tops and asked them which of the teams they had been playing with. Francie Grehan and Nigel Dineen were sitting there that evening with the lads and despite not having a single hurl between them, they confirmed that they had just beaten Kildare.

I think they even managed to get a round of drink on the house for their hurling performance!

WITH TOMMY GONE, some of those senior players wanted myself and players in similar situations to return to the fold. The only problem was that I hadn't trained with the team for a few weeks and my fitness levels had dropped off substantially. That didn't stop our new caretaker manager Val Daly from recalling me to the panel that summer, however. In a strange twist, it would later turn out that Tommy had recommended Val, who had been part of his backroom team, for the caretaker role when he stepped down. I can't think of too many other counties where that would happen.

Recommendation in hand, the Galway man took over for the two remaining games in the league that year, against Longford and Leitrim, before leading us into the Connacht championship.

Our league form had been dismal, and we once again failed to gain promotion, meaning that we would be playing our football in Division 2A in 2006. Only London and Clare had collected fewer points than us that year and teams like Carlow, Leitrim and Longford had finished above us. Was it any wonder even I didn't want to watch us? As disappointing as we had been, I was delighted to be back in the panel. I had been training with the club that year, but it would take time to get back to county level. Hard work didn't bother me though and I hit the gym hard so that I'd be ready when called upon.

OUR CHAMPIONSHIP BEGAN in Ruislip with what was expected to be a routine game against London. I don't know whether it was complacency, loss of confidence or the managerial change, but we were dreadful that day. London deserved to take our scalp and were only the width of a crossbar away from doing so.

They led by two points at half-time after Shane McInerney had punched to the net in the first-half. The half-time team talk didn't stem the tide and Cake was forced to make a vital save just after the restart to save our blushes and keep us in the championship. In the end, we just about scraped through by a point, but there are Roscommon supporters who still remember the crossbar shaking after Scott Doran nearly punched a goal with three minutes left to play. We had survived but the signs were not good.

I was in the wars again in the run-up to that match in London.

I had broken a finger while playing for St Brigid's and had it in a splint which meant missing a couple of weeks of training. It wasn't ideal preparation and a setback I could really have done without.

The broken finger and the lack of match fitness meant that I would once again be on the bench for our semi-final against John Maughan's Mayo at Dr Hyde Park. I could understand the decision to start me on the bench that day, but I hoped to get on early enough to be able to stamp myself on the game.

We started well too and had lots of the ball in the opening half without really opening Mayo up. I was once again struggling as a spectator and grew increasingly frustrated as the game went on and the likes of Ciaran McDonald, Andy Moran and Conor Mortimer began to dictate the tempo.

Val finally brought me on as a last throw of the dice with about 10 minutes to go, but by that stage the game had already drifted away from us. It was a bit degrading really, to be introduced to a team on the brink of a heavy beating and I was angry as I made my way off the pitch at the end.

DALY HAD BROUGHT in the former Roscommon footballer Seamus Killoran as a selector that year and it's fair to say that he and I did not see eye to eye.

As I made my way off the pitch after yet another Mayo drubbing, I saw Killoran approaching. All the pent-up frustration from the previous few months finally came out. 'Why the f**k didn't you bring me on earlier?' I barked.

It had nothing to do with Killoran really, I just wanted to be on the pitch fighting for Roscommon instead of watching us bend the knee to Mayo. It hurt watching them celebrate on our pitch.

There were reports later on that our argument had escalated back in the dressing-room and that we had to be separated, but I have no recollection of it being that bad. Seamus was well able to speak up for himself and he had shot back at me out on the pitch. I then returned fire with a few expletives and walked off.

It wasn't a big deal. Not to me anyway.

Val Daly obviously saw it differently, however, and I received a phone call while delivering post in Kilrooskey on the Monday. Val wanted a few words about what had happened with Seamus the day before – and I wanted to know why he hadn't brought me on earlier in the game.

I could tell straight away from his tone that he had no interest in discussing the substitution though. Instead, he told me I was being dropped for disciplinary reasons after my row with Killoran. It was pure bullshit really.

Lads who were happy to sit on the bench while Mayo laughed at us? That could never be me and I made that clear to him. I loved my county and wanted to fight for it. It was too late. His mind was made up.

The signal kept coming and going throughout our call and we were eventually cut off. I moved the van further down the road where the reception was better and sat there waiting for him to call me back. I felt the onus was on him because the conversation hadn't really finished. I didn't hear from him again that day.

I'll admit I had lost my temper with Seamus that day, but I didn't feel like our relationship was beyond repair. We were all grown-ups and sometimes harsh words are exchanged between players and management. Things are said in the heat of the moment. I still don't believe I had overstepped the mark in a big way and my frustration with how the year was going could probably have been taken into account.

There was plenty of anger around the county after that weekend and I was back in the local and national press for all the wrong reasons once again. One of the local journalists even claimed that I was the first GAA player to be dropped twice in the same year. That simply wasn't true. I had walked away from Tommy Carr's panel ahead of the Carlow game and I probably should have employed the same tactic when confronted with Seamus Killoran that Sunday.

I still think the argument was blown out of all proportion and that some members of the media just relished having something to write about. Maybe it kept Roscommon football interesting throughout the year, because sadly there usually wasn't much to write about as the summer went on.

What annoyed us as players though were the opinion pieces that would pop up spouting criticism after poor results and even calling for players to be dropped. Some of these reporters had tipped us to win just the week before and suddenly everything had changed because they had got it wrong. Unfortunately, it was just something you got used to when playing for Roscommon.

I CAN'T IMAGINE what it's like these days with social media. There are barstool experts everywhere on Twitter and Facebook, not to mention those anonymous keyboard warriors. But for all the criticism of certain players, I always believed that a long-term plan and a proper managerial appointment would have saved Roscommon a lot of heartache over the years.

Just think of all the young talent that was around the county not long after 2005. We had lads who won All-Ireland minor medals and a club about to compete with the very best Connacht and Ireland had to offer.

It should have been the start of something special.

« CHAPTER 13 »

MY COUNTY CAREER could have taken a completely different path in 2005, if I had accepted Páidí Ó Sé's invitation to join up with the Westmeath panel following my departure from the Roscommon set-up.

I had agreed to meet the Kerry legend in Bracken's of Kinnegad soon after my withdrawal from Tommy Carr's panel. Our chat had been arranged through one of my cousins on the Athlone side.

The meeting with Páidí probably happened too soon because I was still a bit raw over what had happened with Roscommon and the last thing I wanted was to upset the supporters. I didn't want to seem ungrateful though, so I said I'd head to Kinnegad to hear the man out.

PÁIDÍ WASN'T ONE for beating around the bush and he told me straight out that he wanted me to become part of the Westmeath panel. It was still only midweek but there was a good crowd in Bracken's that night, back when the Celtic Tiger was still in full roar.

To be honest, it was a surreal feeling to be sitting there with Páidí Ó Sé and his driver.

I remember there was a constant flow of sandwiches coming out from the kitchen and Páidí was busy tucking into them. He was a gas man and great company. I was tempted to take him up on his offer because I felt we would have worked well together.

We spoke about Westmeath's brilliant Leinster campaign the year before as well as my situation with Roscommon and my links to the Lake County. He also questioned me about my decision to quit county football and listened when I explained how hard I had worked earlier in the year.

He understood the frustration and seemed sympathetic.

'It'd be a shame to see you finish up,' he said in between sandwiches. 'But it's up to you at the end of the day.'

'Well, Páidí... it's simple really. I'm not working like a dog to sit on the bench.'

I think he got me and appreciated the fact that I just wanted to play football. We were well past the stage where I needed to prove myself and I told him that some managers had got the wrong impression of me.

We must have chatted for well over an hour about football and life in general that night. It remains one of the most enjoyable football chats I've ever had and an evening I'll always remember.

I WAS TORN for a couple of weeks over what to do. I had strong links to Westmeath. I had gone to school in Athlone, played soccer there and later worked and socialised in the town too. Not to mention that my father, uncles and cousins had all represented Westmeath – it would have made a lot of sense for me to follow in their footsteps. I probably had more of a connection to the county than I did to Roscommon in some ways.

A big part of me did want to go for it, but mainly because I still wanted to play county football. The opportunity to play for a manager like Páidí didn't come along very often either and I was seriously flattered that he had taken the time to meet with me.

I mulled it over for a few days but in the end I believe I made the right decision in turning down his offer. It was just too soon, and the hurt caused by my departure from the Roscommon panel was still far too raw. If Páidí had come back the following year it may have been a different story.

The great man wasn't prepared to give up on me straight away, mind you, and he hounded me for a couple of weeks after our meeting. There were plenty of missed calls on my phone because I just didn't have the courage to answer him. I was afraid that if I picked it up, he would've talked me into togging out!

Much like the Rossies, Páidí and Westmeath would have a poor year in 2005. They were beaten by Kildare in the Leinster quarter-finals and then went out of the championship in round two of the qualifiers to Clare. I couldn't help wondering whether I would have made a difference for them. I guess we'll never know.

The opportunity to represent Westmeath would present itself once more in 2007 when another Kerryman, Tomás O'Flatharta enquired about my availability. We met up in my cousin Gary's house in Moate. Both Gary and Dessie were on the Westmeath team at the time and I was desperate to link up with them at that stage.

Tomás though kept his cards really close to his chest during that period and I remember an interview he gave that January just after Westmeath's O'Byrne Cup win. He admitted that there had been lots of speculation but that I wasn't training with Westmeath and no transfer papers had yet been signed. The chairman of the Westmeath County Board also denied that they had been in contact with me.

At least Tomás completely disagreed with then Roscommon manager John Maughan's assessment that I was 'too old' for county football. The Westmeath manager reckoned that at 28, I still had plenty of top-level football in me.

Tomás was also aware of my desire and my eligibility to play for Westmeath and shortly after our meeting in Moate, we met with the secretary of the Westmeath County Board Paddy Collins at Cusack Park in Mullingar. We had a long chat and by the end of it both men seemed quite keen to have me on board.

There was one sticking point, however, according to Paddy.

'You'll have to move clubs.'

'No way. I'm happy with St Brigid's… I can't uproot again,' I told him.

'Well, leave it with me and I'll see if there's a way around it,' he assured me.

It was disappointing that it wasn't as easy as just signing on the dotted line, but I remained hopeful that something could be done, and I could still become a Westmeath player.

UNFORTUNATELY, THE MOVE just never materialised, and it was down to that sticking point Paddy had mentioned. I was dead set against leaving St Brigid's again. I felt we were on the cusp of something great and I wanted to be part of it. The club came first and it's something I've never regretted.

There was another route I could have taken to make the switch possible but even the thought of it was worse than the idea of leaving Kiltoom. According to another one of their officials, I could play for Westmeath if I was willing to declare it as my native county.

Basically, I would have to state on record that I regarded myself as a Westmeath man rather than a Roscommon one. That was never going to happen. I may have had plenty of disagreements with managers and officials over the years, but as the Waterford hurler John Mullane once said… 'I love me county!'

I loved nothing more than pulling on that primrose and blue jersey and representing Roscommon.

IT WAS UNFORTUNATE that relations had broken down with Roscommon over the years and I felt no other option but to walk away. I don't think it would happen these days. Back then, managers could almost run a dictatorship and there was little an out-of-favour player could do. There is no doubt that I was outspoken and difficult at times, but at the heart of that was a burning desire to see Roscommon succeed.

While there had been huge uncertainty around my Roscommon career in 2005, I had at last found some stability at club level. The success of our underage teams had finally started to translate into success at senior level and every year we seemed to have exciting players breaking through.

Ger Dowd was in charge of us ahead of the 2005 season. Ger has always been well respected at the club, so much so that I brought him in as part of my backroom 11 years later in 2016.

A lot had happened since our last county title win in 1997. If someone had told us back then then we wouldn't manage to get our hands on another senior championship for eight years, I think we would have laughed in their face.

There were a few near misses between 1997 and 2005, of course, including a shock defeat to Kilbride in 2000 and two final defeats in 2002 and '03. The Kilbride defeat in 2000 was made a little bit easier to take knowing great men like the Lohan brothers and John Hanley got a taste of success. By 2005 though, our run had developed into a mini-famine and it was about time we put that right.

There was huge belief around the club at that time.

We were all very much aware that we had a special group of players. There was a feeling that we were finally able to challenge regularly and that was mainly down to the emergence of lads like Karol Mannion, Ian and Senan Kilbride, Mark O'Carroll, Darragh Donnelly, Robbie Kelly, Niall Grehan and others. The floodgates had opened from our minor and under-21 teams and now it was all about keeping expectations in check as these boys became men.

We ended our eight-year wait for a county title by beating Pádraig Pearses in the final in 2005. It was expected to be a tight game but, in the end, we were fairly comfortable and ran out winners by four points. John Tiernan grabbed both of our goals.

This Brigid's team was much different to the one which had claimed county honours back in 1997 and the so the wild celebrations of that week were not repeated in Kiltoom in 2005. Don't get me wrong, we did celebrate but we decided to skip the late-night trip to Skibbereen! There were bigger challenges on the horizon now, and we were determined to take the Connacht championship seriously.

WHILE EVERYTHING HAD gone to plan in Roscommon, our Connacht club semi-final against Leitrim champions Kiltubrid showed us that we would not have it all our own way in the province. They frustrated us in the first game up in Carrick-on-Shannon and equalised deep into second-half injury-time to earn a replay in Kiltoom. It was a dreadful game which ended nine points apiece.

We knew we had a point to prove back in Kiltoom but the Leitrim champions were a stubborn side. It was another tough afternoon, but I managed to score seven points, while Karol Mannion hit a goal and two points, and we finally got the job done. My old minor teammate John Tiernan was impressive again that day too.

It was a relief to know that despite all the young bucks coming through, there was still a place for us auld fellas!

That win set up a Connacht final against the Galway side Salthill-Knocknacarra in Salthill and that was a game that really opened our eyes to the amount of work we still had to do to be able to compete at that level. We were annihilated that day. The highlight for me was probably the half-time break when Cake got his hands on Ger Dowd's manager's diary. Cake was making an emotional speech to us and he decided it would be a good idea to rip every page out of the diary.

The pages were all over the dressing-room floor.

I was thinking… *Poor Ger!*

I thought Ger might have a breakdown, because that diary was like a bible to him – and there was Cake ripping it to pieces, froth coming out of his mouth almost. I still can't lie… it was hard not to burst out laughing!

Salthill had Michael Donnellan, Maurice Sheridan and Alan Kerins playing and we just couldn't handle them. By the full-time whistle, the gap was eight points, but it felt wider than that.

I had a poor game and apart from one point from a free, contributed little. But as a team we just weren't at Salthill's level, physically or mentally.

Michael Donnellan was one of the best players I've ever shared a pitch with, and he was untouchable that day. We've come up against each other a few times and we've also been teammates for Connacht. He's a class act and was part of a brilliant Salthill team that went on to win the All-Ireland club title the following year.

With our season over, we went on the beer after that defeat in order to lick our wounds. The mood wasn't great among the players and the optimism from our county title win had long gone. Salthill had felt like a humiliation and we knew that there was a real gulf in class between them and us.

We were disheartened but it wasn't long before each player was asking the same question… *What do we have to do to get to that level?* We were never going to be satisfied with Roscommon titles.

Some of our younger players had grown used to beating all-comers at underage level so that winning mentality was there. That Brigid's team was always destined for great things, we just needed to take the next step.

I've always believed the foundations for the success we had in the years that followed were laid that year. The lads had huge ambition, but that hammering in Salthill was the kick in the backside needed to really focus minds.

We realised we had to bridge the gap both psychologically and physically and we had to do it fast. From then on, we trained harder than ever before and started to look for challenge games against some of the better teams around the country.

There was no point cruising it in Roscommon. We needed to be taken out of our comfort zone.

THOSE CHALLENGE MATCHES really opened our eyes, especially the games against the Dublin clubs. Their fitness levels were off the charts and they were always physically strong too. We thought we were flying in training, until we came up against those Dublin boys!

It felt like we were chasing shadows at times. They would just keep moving the ball at pace and you'd be getting dizzy trying to keep up. Walking off at the full-time whistle thinking… *F**k, these boys are like machines.* It was the level we wanted to reach; the only question was how could we possibly get there?

It was way above anything any of us had experienced before and it became our mountain to climb over the next few years.

I would have plenty of time to think about club football in the years that followed. I was cast into the county wilderness in 2005 when our Mayo tormentor from a few years before, John Maughan was handed the reins of the Roscommon senior team.

One of Maughan's first moves was to drop several senior players, including myself, Shane Curran, Nigel Dineen, Francie Grehan and Michael 'Mixer' Ryan. It was a bold move and one that is still difficult to make sense of. Shane Curran had been the team captain the previous year.

Did he do it to improve harmony in the panel… or did he do it simply to show everyone who was boss?

Surely it was more important to give himself the best possible chance of winning?

Personally speaking, I think he overestimated the strength of the panel back then and thought he could do without the players he considered troublemakers. As a manager, I would always want to give myself the best chance of success and to do that you need your best players available, especially in a smaller county like Roscommon.

Giving Maughan the benefit of the doubt for a moment, perhaps it was his way of starting with a fresh slate. The 'Famous Five' though saw it as a sign of weakness that he couldn't chance having big personalities in the dressing-room.

I think that assessment turned out to be fairly accurate judging by his two years in charge.

Could it have something to do with his army background and the need for a clear chain of command? Maybe.

Were his concerns about us justified? I don't believe they were, and I think his decision drove Roscommon football back a few years.

MAUGHAN MAYBE SPOKE about the Roscommon job with Tommy Carr and maybe Tommy warned him about the dangers of player power within the set-up.

Maybe he had a point, but we made no apologies that as senior Roscommon players we always demanded the best from each other as well as the management team. There was an expectation on the manager and his backroom team that they would make every tool at their disposal available to us to improve us as a team.

Was that too much to ask?

WHATEVER ABOUT MAUGHAN'S reasoning, I'll never forget the day I found out that I was no longer considered part of the county panel.

I was sitting in my car having just left a sports shop in Golden Island Shopping Centre in Athlone after buying a new pair of football boots. The radio was tuned to *Shannonside FM* when the sports news came on and it was announced that the new Roscommon manager was ringing the changes.

I came awfully close to flinging the new Adidas Predators out the window in disgust. The b*****d had hung my boots up before I had even taken them out of the box!

I was devastated by the news, but I was also angry that the new man hadn't bothered to get in touch with me himself. If you're going to make the decision to end a player's county career, at least have the courage and the decency to pick up the phone.

Later, he would confirm that his management team didn't believe I was at the required standard for county football. Talk about kicking a man when he's down! This was even though I was still representing Connacht in the Railway Cup.

I must have been one the very few players to get picked for his province but not for his county. My form with St Brigid's would eventually force him to have a rethink but for now, I was surplus to requirements.

John Maughan doesn't deserve all of the blame for dropping the five of us, however. It all comes back to the absence of a long-term vision for Roscommon football as well as some interference from former players.

It was well known within the county panel that certain past players held a regular conclave to discuss the current status of the Roscommon senior team. I'm sure they probably still do. They carried far too much influence at times for men whose time had come and gone a couple of decades before.

The county board was at fault too and certain members must take responsibility for the lack of success the Roscommon team achieved during that era. It would be 2010 before the county won another Connacht title. That simple fact tells you all you need to know about how things were being run.

SOMETHING STILL DOESN'T feel right about the whole thing. Dropping experienced players was the equivalent of Maughan tying his own hands before his stint had even begun. Would it have been allowed to happen in any other county? Why were he and his management team allowed to end the county careers of five players? A Mayo man, or any man from outside a county, making that decision about Roscommon footballers, to me that seems wrong! I was effectively being retired at 27 years of age – our county board got away lightly by allowing this to happen. After all the years of service all of us had given our county? I'm still in dismay at how it was allowed to happen.

I do think there was a small minority on that panel who would have been happy enough to see the back of us though. It's no coincidence that the five who were dropped would go on to become managers or coaches. We knew the game and we demanded high standards, during training and matches. It seemed to me that some of the other lads on that panel just didn't want the hardship.

Attitudes have certainly changed when it comes to the Roscommon senior team over the years – and changed for the better. Back then, there were lads who were satisfied with being part of the panel. They were happy to be called county players without consistently reaching the standards required.

Put it another way... they were happy to have their initials on the official gear and to strut about in Rockford's on Saturday or Sunday night. They were never going to win you titles or even tough championship matches, and the evidence is there from our results in those years.

THERE WERE REAL leaders and men of character in the Roscommon teams I was part of. Players like Francie, Mixer Ryan, Nigel, Cake, Clifford McDonald, Gary Cox... Fergie O'Donnell. If your performance wasn't up to scratch or you weren't putting the work in at training, then those guys wouldn't be slow in letting you know.

That's exactly what any ambitious player would want, and it was something I relished.

Every player is different, and some seemed content just getting splinters on their backsides every Sunday while watching on from the bench.

It must also be remembered that there was a great deal of excitement in the county during the Maughan years, due to the quality of our minor team.

In 2006, Fergal O'Donnell famously led the youngsters to All-Ireland glory against Kerry in Ennis. It was a day that will live forever in the folklore of Roscommon GAA and there was a real feel-good factor around football in the county afterwards.

A proper long-term plan would have seen those young players being carefully blooded into the senior set-up over the following years. To my mind, they weren't ready to make that step up straight away and had a lot of developing still to do.

There is a real danger that you ruin a young player by exposing him to senior action too early. Some players are more resilient than others and looking back at my own career, I am glad I was held back at the start.

After wielding his axe, Maughan then had to drop some of the more inexperienced players in at the deep end. He had denied them a golden opportunity to learn and develop alongside the likes of Francie Grehan, Shane Curran, 'Mixer' and Nigel Dineen. Top men who would have offered guidance as well as protection in the choppy waters of senior county football.

Nobody will ever convince me that Roscommon wouldn't have been better off with those men inside the tent. Right or wrong, the Roscommon footballing public puts huge pressure on its players and management. Some from outside the county would accuse us of having delusions of grandeur at times but we have a proud footballing tradition, and we expect to compete.

However, for those young players who had just toppled The Kingdom to become All-Ireland champions, the pressure would only intensify. That level of expectation makes those all-important development years even more difficult.

I've always been a firm believer that unless a player has exceptional talent and is physically resilient then the 'softly, softly' approach should be applied. Utilising the underage structures to ease a player into the senior set-up is the most prudent pathway.

Even a generational talent such as Kerry's David Clifford wasn't just thrown into the action as part of an inexperienced team. There were seasoned veterans to guide him so that he could develop and find his feet.

IN FAIRNESS TO John Maughan, his first league campaign that year ended with five wins from seven as Roscommon narrowly missed out on promotion. Though it was a weak Division 2A which featured the likes of London, Carlow, Clare and Longford. Donegal were the pick of the bunch.

His first taste of the Connacht championship was a comfortable win in New York before Galway fought back from a half-time deficit to win an entertaining semi-final at Dr Hyde Park. Roscommon's championship involvement that year ended with a 13-point hammering by Meath in Navan in round two of the qualifiers.

If 2006 was an underwhelming start to life under John Maughan, 2007 was an absolute disaster. That Roscommon team was making a habit of throwing away good leads and capitulating in the second-half of games.

The year was over after defeat to Kildare in the qualifiers.

Meanwhile, it was only a matter of time before the door was flung open and I was lacing up those Adidas Predators for county training once more.

PART FIVE

Fruit of Kiltoom

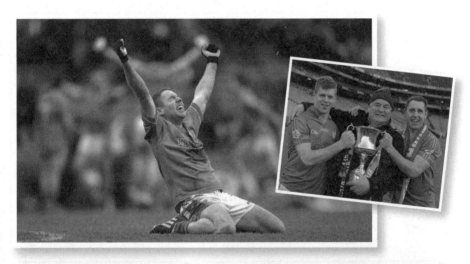

« CHAPTER 14 »

PRIOR TO HIS success with Galway and Roscommon, Anthony Cunningham was working his magic in Kiltoom and Athlone. The Galway native was appointed St Brigid's manager in 2006 and he guided us to yet another Roscommon title that year. It was our eighth title in all and while we still trailed the likes of Clann na nGael on the county's roll of honour, there had been a major shift in power in Roscommon football.

Things had changed at the club over the years and our devastating defeat in the previous year's Connacht final meant that the players were driving new standards in the dressing-room Cunningham entered in 2006.

OUR COUNTY FINAL win over St Faithleach's that year didn't really tell the full story of our dominance in the Roscommon championship. Faithleach's made things very tough for us but a goal from Garvan helped us on our way to a narrow 1-7 to 1-5 win. It also kept our feet firmly on the ground for bigger challengers ahead. No longer were we content with county titles – it was time to take the next step a win our first Connacht crown.

'Dramatic' would be the word I'd use to describe our Connacht campaign that year. It started unconvincingly enough with a narrow 1-9 to 1-8 win over Sligo champions Curry in the preliminary round, thanks to a David O'Connor goal and a late point from Senan Kilbride.

Mayo champions Crossmolina Deel Rovers were the favourites for the Shane McGettigan Cup that year. They had won the All-Ireland Club Championship in 2001 and were a strong outfit. We were boosted by the fact that both the semi-final and final of that year's competition were played at the Hyde and we made full use of home advantage by beating Crossmolina by four points.

The visitors had been wasteful at times, but we had done our homework in the build-up and it helped that John O'Mahony was part of our backroom. He had studied the Mayo champions closely when working with Ballaghaderreen.

Crossmolina had a super team back then, including the likes of Ciaran McDonald, James and Tom Nallen, and Peadar Gardiner. Our determination to get over the line could be seen right up to the final whistle that day, when 13 of us raced back to stand on the line as McDonald looked for a late goal – Ciaran Mac scored a cracker of a goal in a previous game from about 30 yards, so we were ready and prepared for him to try it again.

We were ready to do whatever it took to win.

Despite that win, we were still the underdogs going into the final showdown with Galway's Corofin, in what was to be the most dramatic game of our campaign.

Corofin made a late change in the build-up by bringing in Emmett Killeen in place of their captain Alan O'Donovan in their attack. That sticks out in my mind because Killeen was sent off after just five minutes for an off the ball tussle with Donal O'Connor. So much for best laid plans!

Even with 14 men Corofin were formidable and managed to cut through us for two early goals. We did get a bit of a foothold after that and the half-time score saw us lead with seven points to their two goals.

THE SECOND-HALF was one of most dramatic 30-minute periods I've ever been involved in. Corofin were well on top when Robbie Kelly was sent off and they built up a two-point lead by injury-time at the end of the game, after their captain Alan O'Donovan came on and converted a penalty.

It was much closer than the Salthill game the year before, but it was beginning to look like it was curtains for us once again.

Step forward Karol Mannion. After the game, 'Mango' would claim that he was at fault for two of the Corofin goals. If that was the case, then Karol more than made up for it with a bit of magic right at the end to win us our first-ever Connacht title.

We were desperately chasing a goal deep into injury-time when the ball was worked to Mango on the left wing. We looked on as he cut inside and hit an absolute screamer past Glen Comer in the Corofin goal. It was bedlam all over the Hyde when that one went in!

I think I was still in shock at the full-time whistle but the scenes among our supporters were something else. You couldn't have written a better script for a final and there was no player more deserving than Karol Mannion when it came to being Brigid's' hero that day.

Despite being one of the best footballers in the club's history, he remains one of the humblest men I've ever had the pleasure of knowing too. The way he put his hands up to claim responsibility for their goals told you everything you needed to know about him.

I NEVER REALLY expected us to go on and challenge the likes of Corofin when it came to the amount of Connacht titles won after we beat them at the Hyde. But we did enjoy a good bit of success in the province and what we learned under managers like Ger Dowd and Anthony Cunningham stood to us in the years that followed.

We had leaders all over the field too. Cake in goal, Mango and Garvan in midfield, and the likes of me and Senan in the forward line. It was like having managers all over the pitch in many ways. The managers we had didn't have to do an awful lot once we stepped over the white line and that's something that I've tried to drill into my own teams nowadays.

Very few of the sideline instructions are absorbed while the game is going on anyway so it's better that guidance comes from players in the thick of the action.

It also helped that our managers during that time trusted us. There wasn't a lot of discussion in terms of tactics compared to what's going on now. It was more of a case of going out and playing the game.

Off the field, an 'alcohol ban' was never officially introduced at St Brigid's but players knew not to drink the week of a game. You would normally be off it anyway when training.

We trained every Wednesday and Friday, and Sunday morning, and that was

Gospel. There was no such thing back then as WhatsApp or group messages, you knew when the sessions were on and it was up to you to be there.

As players, we maintained high standards and that started with training and was then carried into games. Those sessions were more difficult than many of our matches because we demanded every last drop of effort from one another.

We expected the younger players coming through to buy into all of this too and if they didn't, they wouldn't last very long on the panel anyway. The team had to be more important than any one player.

It all paid off and I think we had a panel that was a few levels above anything else in Roscommon for a few years. Even our substitutes were confident of competing for a county title. We blew teams out of the water in most of our games. We did have a few scares along the way too but even the best teams ride their luck sometimes.

While Anthony Cunningham deserves great credit for encouraging the discipline and high standards that saw us go on to dominate in both Roscommon and Connacht, he was also an excellent man manager and someone who trusted us as adults.

I remember one incident when Anthony had organised a recovery session for whoever wanted it in the swimming pool at the Hodson Bay Hotel after we won the county final. Myself and Garvan were out celebrating in Daly's Tavern while most of the lads were down in the pool.

At one stage, I looked at the watch and said we should head down and show our faces. Garvan was a bit reluctant, but we got a lift off one of the lads in the pub and asked him to hang around for a few minutes in the hotel car park while we went in and had a chat with Anthony and the others.

When we arrived in the changing rooms some of the lads had already finished and were getting dressed to leave. There was no sign of Cunningham.

'Where's Anto?'

'Still in the steam room.'

There was no point in coming all that way and the man himself not seeing the effort we had made! We decided to stick our heads in for a quick chat.

Now, bear in mind that we had been on the beer for two days solid, and we were now sitting in the steam room fully dressed, with Anthony Cunningham and other members of the team sitting across from us.

Thankfully, he didn't seem to mind and was pleased that we had made the effort to be there. Or maybe he just couldn't really see us with all the steam. Mission accomplished… off we went back to Daly's with our clothes stuck to us!

OUR FIRST TILT at the All-Ireland Club Championship in 2007 was brought to an abrupt end by the Armagh and Ulster champions Crossmaglen. They were a formidable outfit and they ground us down in our semi-final in Mullingar. We didn't play well as a team that day and Cross beat us by a goal.

It was hugely disappointing after all the hard work we had put in over the previous year. We trained like lunatics at the army barracks in Athlone that Christmas and there was a real feeling of belief around the camp. We were in incredible shape and unstoppable through the Roscommon and Connacht championships.

Our defeat to Crossmaglen was a tough one to take and there was more pain ahead as the team entered a bit of a transition period after that defeat. It would be four years before any of us reached that level again.

« CHAPTER 15 »

I WAS BUSY delivering post on the outskirts of Roscommon town in early 2007 when I first laid eyes on her. From that point on, I'd meet her walking out the road in the mornings and quickly discovered that her parents lived on the Racecourse Road.

It was an instant attraction, well on my part anyway!

We hadn't spoken much at this point, but I made sure the post always arrived to the Gannon's house around the same time each morning just in case.

It was time to find out more about the dark-haired beauty driving the red Ford Focus so I did what any good brother would do, and I enlisted my sister Kara as a spy.

And that's pretty much how I first came to know Caroline Gannon.

We shared brief conversations in the weeks that followed until we finally got chatting properly at Rockfords in Roscommon one night.

Caroline's payslips were still being sent to her home house at that stage and her mother Aideen had asked me if we could reroute them to her daughter's new address in Ashbrook. It maybe wasn't the smoothest topic to break the ice with, but it seemed to work!

We chatted for a while that night before I asked her out for the first time, and before she shot me down for the first time. I didn't give up on her straight away though and continued to chat to her in the weeks that followed. But it was clear that there was serious reluctance on her part!

How reluctant was she?

Well, Caroline tells a story about the time she had travelled to Boston for a cousin's wedding. She was staying at the home of Nuala and Paddy O'Sullivan, who are related to Caroline's extended family. Nuala's maiden name is Coyle, and she is originally from Curraghboy. She pointed to a picture of some St Brigid's corner-forward she had on her fridge, teasing Caroline.

'Have you still not found yourself a nice Kiltoom man, like this one?'

Caroline took one look at the picture and was completely unimpressed.

'No thanks, you're alright!'

It was always going to take a bit of time for the man on the fridge to get past Caroline's cold shoulder!

The breakthrough finally arrived around six months later when she agreed to go to the cinema in Athlone. The plan was that she would collect me in Kiltoom and we'd head in together. I thought just the one pint in Daly's would surely settle those first date nerves!

The craic and pints were flowing in Daly's in the company of Ray Nestor that night however, and one pint quickly became two. Caroline pulled up outside to collect me for our date but by then a night in the cinema held little appeal.

Plus, I figured we'd get to know each other better over a few drinks. It proved to be the right decision because we both had a great night and it's been going well ever since.

BEFORE I MET Caroline, I had been reluctant to get involved in serious relationships because of my commitment to Gaelic football. There just wasn't any time for much else aside from work, training and matches.

Playing for St Brigid's and Roscommon was like a full-time job in itself at times – I can only imagine what it's like for modern day players.

Meeting Caroline changed everything.

She wasn't just any girl and I was at an age, 29, when it was time to think about getting serious and settling down. It also helped that I had more time on my hands without Roscommon commitments. Not that my football skills or a Roscommon career would have impressed Caroline anyway!

No matter what has happened on or off the pitch in the years that have followed,

Caroline has been the one constant. She is great at keeping my feet firmly on the ground. Her support has been amazing, and she has shown remarkable patience when it comes to me missing weddings and other big family events on account of my football.

There have been times when Caroline has had to attend weddings alone due to a match. There has even been the odd occasion when a challenge match has taken priority over a family event.

Football came first and it's something Caroline was forced to come to terms with. Was it fair? Probably not, but that was the level of my obsession with the game.

I HAD BOUGHT a house in Athlone just before we started going out and had moved into it just as the relationship was becoming serious. Like many people approved for a mortgage during the Celtic Tiger era, home ownership and the debts that came with it quickly became a constant source of stress. I'm still paying for that house even though I no longer own it and it's something that has been on my mind since buying it.

I probably shouldn't have been given a mortgage in the first place and I'm lucky that I received some good advice from Eamon O'Rourke. But it was something that hung over me for a few years and it added to my worries.

Playing football was a welcome release during that period in my life and it gave me a bit of head space. When I was on the pitch I just thought about football. Any of the problems I've ever had were quickly put to the back of my mind when there was a ball to be won or a point to be scored.

The problem with using football as a distraction is that the problem never really goes away. I'd be back thinking about my financial worries and other problems as soon as I got into the shower after a match or training.

Things are much better now, and I consider myself to be one of the lucky ones. There were many people who fell into that trap during the carefree credit days of the Celtic Tiger and some didn't make it out. It was a crazy time in this country and one that should be used as a lesson to young people today.

Ten years have passed but there are still people paying for homes from that era. The approach to lending has caused huge long-term problems for this country and at the end of the day, it's always the ordinary working people who suffer.

WHILE CAROLINE HAD grabbed my attention off the pitch, there was still plenty to distract me when it came to St Brigid's in 2007. That was the year I captained the club to its first-ever three in-a-row of Roscommon senior football titles. Brigid's had given me a great platform ever since John Maughan decided I wasn't up to county standards and I was really enjoying my football again.

I had adapted my game over the previous two or three years and was now comfortable as a creative force further out the field. There was still something missing though, and I felt I was too young to close the door completely on Roscommon.

Not being one to remain quiet on a topic for too long, I used our victory after the county final in 2007 to call on Maughan and his management team to select the best players available to give the county a real crack at being a force in Connacht again. It was common knowledge even before that final that I wanted to be back playing for Roscommon. I had given an interview to the local papers as part of our preview night and let it be known that I was ready.

I had swallowed my pride and was now pleading to be called in from the cold. It hurt seeing my county struggle so badly against teams we should have been beating.

The ball was now in John Maughan's court.

Sure enough, just a few days after our county final win, I was in Caroline's house when the phone rang. I didn't recognise the number, so it was a surprise when John Maughan introduced himself. I hadn't heard from John since he was appointed in 2005. He made it clear that day on the phone the level of commitment needed to be part of his Roscommon panel.

He didn't need to tell me how tough it would be. I was looking forward to the challenge. But, in the meantime, I was busy preparing for yet another Connacht Club Championship with St Brigid's.

Anthony Cunningham was certainly getting a tune out of us at that stage and we looked set to retain our Connacht title when we hammered Padraic Joyce's Killererin side in our semi-final in Tuam.

For the record, it was Joyce who made the headlines with a Man of the Match display and a total of a goal and nine points. He was a class player, but he could do nothing about our attack where David O'Connor was on form. He got two goals that day, but it could have been four.

Senan Kilbride, Cathal McHugh and Karol Mannion were also impressive, while I converted four frees and was involved in a few of our other scores. We were purring along nicely for another Connacht final, this time against Ballina Stephenites in Ballina.

That was a game that just didn't go our way, however.

We should have made it back-to-back titles, but Ballina got an early goal and from then on we were chasing the game. We rallied well in the second-half but despite playing against 14 men, following David O'Mahony's red card, we just couldn't find a way back. David Clarke was in fine form in the Stephenites' goal but we were guilty of some wasteful shooting – me as much as anyone.

It was another tough defeat to take – it always is against Mayo opposition – but there was a feeling that we had the players and the belief to come again.

We were a long time on the road at that stage following our All-Ireland semi-final defeat to Crossmaglen in February of that year. I spent that winter recharging the batteries because I expected the following year to be one of the busiest years of my career, both for club and county.

I RETURNED TO Roscommon training early in 2008, excited to be back involved at county level and looking forward to running out at the Hyde once more for Roscommon.

It was a huge challenge to regain county fitness levels but as a St Brigid's player I had developed a good base level over the previous two years. The faces on the Roscommon panel had changed too since my last call up, but that didn't matter. It felt good to be back.

Unfortunately, those good vibes didn't last long as we struggled to keep our heads above water in Division Two that year. One win from seven games tells its own story but the fact that we conceded 11 goals and 116 points in those games was the most disheartening part.

There was nowhere for any of us to hide, least of all John Maughan. He was gone after we were hammered by my former suitors Westmeath in Kiltoom and relegated to the third tier of the National League.

We had a young team at that time and four of the lads had been allowed to tog out for the Roscommon under-21s the day before, but there was still no excuse for our 11-point hiding. I came on for Cathal Cregg with eight minutes to go but by then it was too late to change the course of the game.

I tried to force a couple of opportunities, but nothing came off. Watching my cousins Des and Gary playing so well only added to my frustration.

I often wondered whether the venue played a part in Maughan's demise. The game had been switched from Dr Hyde Park to Brigid's' home venue that weekend and maybe the hostile reception he received there helped him to make his mind up.

Warming up on the sideline that day was an education in the pressure and strain county managers are forced to work under. John received quite a lot of abuse from a few of the spectators and you just had a feeling that his position had become untenable. He announced his resignation after that match after three years in charge.

I don't think he endeared himself to the Roscommon footballing public in interviews afterwards either. He referred to the supporters at Kiltoom that day as 'customers' on TV. It was in the heat of the moment though and probably understandable considering the abuse he received.

WITH MAUGHAN GONE, the Roscommon managerial merry-go-round showed no signs of slowing down that year and there were to be three further appointments by the time 2008 was finished.

Firstly, former Roscommon footballer Paul Earley would follow his brother and Roscommon legend Dermot into the Roscommon hot seat. Paul came to his county's aid and took over in a caretaker capacity following Maughan's departure.

Just like Dermot, Paul was an impressive leader as well as being a lovely man. He had also enjoyed an excellent playing career, and became the first Irishman recruited to play in Australia with Melbourne Demons in the Victorian Football League. An All Star in 1985, he would also later manage the Irish International Rules team to victory over the Aussies in 2013.

Paul was only with us for our two remaining dead rubber league games, against Dublin and Cavan, and it just wasn't enough time for him to put his own stamp on things. The Roscommon job would once again be up for grabs, which was hardly ideal preparation for the Connacht championship.

While Paul Earley had stepped forward to guide the team through our remaining league commitments, the speculation around the manager's job had been going on even before the ink on John Maughan's resignation letter had dried.

As always, there were plenty of names in contention but there was a feeling among some of the more senior players that the county board would keep the search close to home for our next manager.

My former teammate Michael 'Mixer' Ryan was by then the under-21 manager, and was tipped as the 'chosen one' among some of the lads. Mixer wasn't giving much away though and, for once, there wasn't a peep from anyone involved with the county board.

One of the lads I was working with at An Post at the time would place a few bets every now and then. Mixer was just 30 years old and had just completed his first year with the under-21s. There were other names in the hat and the appointment of the Roscommon Gaels man would have been seen as a major gamble by people who didn't really know him. But still the rumours continued.

I decided it was worth a punt and asked the betting postman to get me a price for Mixer as the next Roscommon manager. I hadn't spoken to Mixer in a while, but we all knew how badly he wanted a crack at senior management.

The Roscommon under-21s' season had already finished by then, so the path was clear for him to take the seniors into the championship.

I wouldn't have had a lot of money in 2008 but I decided it was probably worth the risk. At that stage Mixer was still an outsider, so you could get him at long odds with some bookies, while he wasn't even listed by others.

My man came up with a cunning plan to get a decent price with one of the local bookmakers who hadn't got Mixer listed at that stage. Like Mixer, he wasn't giving much away when he called me that week.

'I've a great story for the bookie. I'll get the money off you and head in.'

Himself and another fella wanted a piece of the action too, so I met him and handed over my stake and between the three of us we had almost two thousand euros. Off he went to the bookies to get us decent odds.

He told me afterwards that the bookie had a little chuckle when he placed the two grand on the counter.

'Where ya going with all that?' he asked.

The postman's plan kicked into action.

'Ah sure, look, it sounds silly now but... I play five-a-side with a group of lads and every year we place a stupid bet with the leftover money from each week. The lads are at me like a bunch of auld wans.

'They want the bet placed before it gets robbed out of the glove box.'

The bookie was laughing at this stage. 'What's the stupid bet this year?'

'There's a few in for the Roscommon manager's job, but the lads used to play a bit with Mick Ryan in town and they wanted to wind him up by showing him the slip. What odds are we talking?'

The bookie gave it some thought and came up with a price for the Roscommon Gaels outsider. It must have been about 9/1.

I WILL NEVER forget pulling into Roscommon training later that week and the sheer joy of seeing Mixer Ryan's car in the carpark. I ran past him and out onto the pitch, flashing him a big cheesy grin. Only delighted to see him.

I'm sure any of the county board officials looking on must have thought… *Jesus Christ, he might actually get on with this one!*

The exact stake and odds are a blur to me now, but we took something in the region of €18,000 out of the bookies that week. We might not have been winning on the pitch but at least some of us were winning off it!

BACK TO THE serious business of training, and I had teamed up with Clann na nGael's Donie Shine to do some extra work. The two of us were making our way back to full fitness following injury. I really enjoyed those sessions with Donie. He had already reached hero status within Roscommon following his performances with the 2006 All-Ireland winning minor team. He would later go on to become a legend for his club before being forced to retire early due to injury.

Donie loved football, and he was a coming force at senior level, with a promising county career spread out in front of him. His performances in 2010 would set him apart as one of the best footballers we've had in the county in the last 20 years. It was just a shame that he didn't get to feature even more for Roscommon.

While Donie's star was just beginning to rise, there was a feeling that my own was beginning to fade on the county stage.

I was named as a substitute for Mixer's first match in charge, a Connacht quarter-final against Galway in Salthill. It was a baptism of fire for Mixer and a harsh introduction to senior county management.

The Tribesmen were in no mood to roll out the red carpet that day and our championship hopes went up in flames as we were hammered up and down the promenade. Gary Cox was also sent off in the 16-point drubbing. The only bright spots from a Roscommon point of view were the championship debuts of Senan Kilbride, Mark O'Carroll and Conor Devaney.

Our defeat in Galway was humiliating and Mixer had a huge job on his hands to pick the players up ahead of the first round of the All-Ireland qualifiers. We were drawn against Donegal in Ballybofey and I didn't even make the bench for that one.

Donegal were far too strong for a Roscommon team whose confidence had been shredded, and they ran out easy winners.

THE RECORD BOOKS will show that Mixer was winless as manager of the Roscommon seniors and people will say that the big job came too early in his career. He was unfortunate with sending offs and injuries, and the Donegal match was a prime example of this. That day we were harshly reduced to 13 men when Cathal Cregg and Johnny Dunning were sent to the line for 'nothing' offences.

Mixer was never a man to let his county down and he stood up at a time when others wouldn't. Unfortunately, results went against him and his short reign ended following that defeat to Donegal.

I felt my time was coming to an end once again too.

Although he had only been in charge for two matches, there had been more communication with Mixer in that time than there had been with any other manager. He was a players' coach, and you knew where you stood with him.

Good man management means talking to players and letting them know exactly what you want from them. Mixer was good at letting you know in a diplomatic way if he didn't think you were fit enough or ready to start.

Some managers and coaches don't handle people well. There were times with Roscommon and Brigid's when I didn't know where I was at with managers. *Were they happy with my performances? Was I doing what they wanted?*

It is first and foremost a team game but being unsure about your own part in that team can be unsettling. It resulted in me trying to do too much in matches rather than focusing on the game plan.

As a manager, it's important to remember that players are human beings who are motivated in different ways. It's your job to bring them together and keep them onside. Sometimes that means biting your tongue. It's all about winning at the elite level, after all.

I've always believed that allowances must be made for certain players too. There are some lads who react to an arm around the shoulder and there are others who need a kick up the backside. There are ways of laying down the law without turning it into a standoff too. Players aren't stupid... well most of them aren't anyway!

Communication is a massive part of management and most lads will get the message even when it's not delivered directly.

I THINK THE communication from management to players could have been much better between 2003 and '08 with Roscommon. It was a different era.

Players are treated like valued employees of a company nowadays and player welfare is first and foremost. The constant chopping and changing in those five years didn't help either, but more could have been done to support players back then. It wasn't all bad though. Managers like Mixer, Gay Sheerin and even Tommy Carr in 2003, would make it clear what they wanted. They also encouraged me to play my natural game which meant that I was confident in my role.

Sometimes tactics don't work, or a player can have an off day, and in knockout football that can heap pressure on the manager. This can lead to overthinking and changes which unsettle the team. Managing a football-mad county is not easy and it requires support from the county board and serious buy-in from the players.

The axe won't be long falling if you lose either.

Personally speaking, I think I was unfortunate to play with so many managers with a Defence Forces background. I've nothing against the army and there were exceptions to the rule, but I just found some of those lads to be too rigid in their dealings with players.

If I had to pick, I'd say Gay Sheerin was the best Roscommon manager I played under because he was someone you could talk to. It also helped that he had Roscommon football's best interests at heart and that we trusted each other. On the other hand, John Tobin was the best coach I played under with Roscommon. He was ahead of his time and with Des Ryan on board training was tough, but enjoyable. They brought us to a new level.

Timing helps too, and Gay was manager at a time when players enjoying themselves after a match was acceptable. The game became far more professional with each passing year after that glorious summer of 2001, as some of us fell out of love along the way.

« CHAPTER 16 »

I HAVE RECEIVED counselling on a couple of occasions. The first time was in 2009 and I hadn't been going out with Caroline for very long at that stage.

One day I just broke down crying. I had no idea why. It was a scary moment.

It was so hard to explain just 'something doesn't feel right here'. I had been a bit down for a while and this feeling had started to gnaw at me. Maybe meeting Caroline triggered something too. It was a new stage of my life and I felt like I was growing up. Was it time to deal with feelings I had bottled up?

I made an appointment to go and chat with a local counsellor. I was nervous heading in there the first day, thinking… *What if someone sees me?* By the end of the session though, it felt like a massive weight had been taken from me. It did me the world of good.

I may appear pure emotional on the football pitch at times, but I wouldn't be the best man to pour out my feelings when it comes to personal stuff. I've played in some big matches against some very tough men but the thoughts of spilling my guts in counselling was scary! My counsellor was excellent though and she helped me to see that one of the reasons I had broken down was my parents' split in 2001 and the problems they had endured long before that. It was something I hadn't really dealt with properly at the time.

It's an unsettling event at any stage of life and leads you to question your own relationships and, of course, sparked those memories from childhood and growing up. Rather than deal with it at the time though, I buried myself in football.

Football was great for that.

As long as I was training or playing a match, I could forget all about the outside world for a while. It didn't matter that the painful feelings would be with me in the car on the way home and stay with me in the days that followed. Football would always give me an hour or two of headspace.

That was fine in the short term, but as time went on the same issues were still floating around and causing me grief. Those bad feelings don't go away unless you get to the bottom of them and the counselling allowed me to bring my fears and worries out into the light where they weren't as scary anymore.

If there is one piece of advice I'd give to young sportspeople, it's to open up and deal with any problems or issues as soon as you can. I see now that I had let mine build up over a period of 10 years until they got on top of me and started to drag me down.

It's only a matter of time before you break under that pressure and that's when a good partner, friend, teammate or family member is worth their weight in gold. I was lucky that I received a lot of support and that helped me to see a way forward.

Caroline played a vital role too. She could see early on that I wasn't myself and she was the one who put the idea of counselling in my head. She also showed a lot of patience because I wasn't very receptive to the idea of talking about my feelings at first.

Like many men, feelings are not something I had ever really spoken about. Maybe after a few pints I'd spill my guts to Caroline or the mother, or even the barman! But talking to the lads or a complete stranger? Forget it!

I don't tend to get too down these days, and I can't say I'm a man who overthinks things a lot. Looking back, I think I did suffer from a bit of depression and I dealt with my issues the same way many Irishmen do, by going off on drinking sessions. I'd go off drinking after matches on a Sunday and then I'd be in work on Monday dealing with the come down.

Between the naked pool episode, the issues with my mother and father, and Sundays spent drinking pints of the ultimate depressant, it was only a matter of time before it all caught up with me.

THERE WERE OTHER times, too, when off-field problems threatened to spill over into football. In 2002, I was out of work after my shoulder injury.

I was borrowing the mother's Nissan Sunny along with 10 euros for petrol just so I could make it to the Roscommon training sessions in Ballyforan. It was tough pulling into the car park and seeing the other lads arriving in from work and that feeling is something that has never left me.

That kind of stuff gave me a crucial insight into why lads might not be themselves at training or why they might be a bit off-form in matches. It's important to consider the human being as well as the athlete.

You just never know what might be going on at home or what sort of baggage a fella is carrying into the dressing-room.

I really was growing up and after years of successfully dodging serious relationships due to football, things had become serious with Caroline in late-2009. I had made my mind up to pop the question and even came up with a romantic plan for the proposal.

We had been to New York together before and loved it. It's an amazing city and the perfect setting for a big romantic gesture. Unless she says no, of course, and you have to request separate seats on the flight home! I've been nervous for football matches before, but nothing like I was on that trip. I decided to use the money I had won on the Mixer Ryan bet to buy her a ring in The Big Apple. Caroline could pick whatever ring she wanted, provided she said yes!

THE PLAN WAS to travel to Boston and then on to New York. What I didn't factor in was how nervous I'd be travelling through three airports with thousands of euros in cash tucked away in my luggage. I was completely stressed from the moment we left the house in Roscommon, until we landed in New York. Talk about ruining the mood. 'What's wrong with you?' Caroline kept asking.

Things got worse the longer our trip went on and my stress must have transferred onto her.

My plan was in tatters by the time we were standing at the top of the Empire State Building with the whole city laid out before us. I tried to pluck up the courage on the viewing platform but dealing with me over the previous few days had clearly put Caroline in bad form.

I looked down at the streets over a hundred floors below and thought I'd be safer popping the question at ground level. Standing in the lift on the way back down, I knew I had bottled it big time.

'Will we go for a drink?' Yeah, some Dutch courage might help!

LATER THAT EVENING, as we came back to ourselves and strolled around the city, I finally proposed. Though for some reason – probably nerves – I asked her if she'd like to get engaged rather than the traditional... 'Will you marry me?'

I didn't even go down on one knee because that felt stupid without the ring.

I remember that we were on our way back to the hotel because we had tickets for *Grease The Musical* on Broadway. We were on 34th Street and I was about to experience my very own miracle.

'Look, this is harder than playing in Croke Park... do you want to get engaged?'

Those were my exact words. Fairytale proposal my arse!

For some reason, Caroline overlooked all that and she said yes straight away. To continue with the comparison to football, it was like hearing the final whistle at the end of a tight county final – one you're winning of course!

To this day, I'm not sure if she knew what was coming and just didn't fancy the idea of being proposed to in front of a crowd of tourists, or whether I had put her in a bad mood by stressing out over the money. It doesn't matter.

The grand 'proposal' happened outside a flower shop on some sidewalk in New York. The shop was closed at the time so I couldn't even redeem myself by grabbing her a bunch of flowers.

It also turned out that we had our dates mixed up, and that night we had tickets to a basketball game and not her favourite Broadway musical. To wrap up our romantic evening, I took her to a Red Lobster for dinner. What a lucky girl!

CAROLINE CALLED HER parents to tell them the good news and I called my mother.

'I knew what you were up to the minute you mentioned New York,' she said.

So much for the element of surprise!

We were both in much better form the following morning and went to pick out Caroline's ring. We could then enjoy a lovely couple of days in New York despite my botched proposal. Caroline confirmed to me that day and many days since that she has the patience of a saint for putting up with me.

WE WERE MARRIED at the Sacred Heart Church in Roscommon around Christmas time in 2010 and had our reception at the Sheraton Hotel in Athlone afterwards. Caroline's father Padraig took great pleasure in telling everyone, in his Father of the Bride speech, how he first came to meet his daughter's new husband.

It turned out that Padraig was an umpire for a few of the referees based in Roscommon town, the likes of Jimmy Reilly and Declan Hunt. He was on duty for a match that I was playing in before I started going out with Caroline.

During this match I swung the ball over the bar, or so I thought. Padraig waved it wide as I made my case strongly, not knowing who he was. He stuck to his guns and the referee agreed, while I raised genuine concern for Padraig's eyesight. I suppose I'll just have to give him the benefit of the doubt at this stage!

WE'VE BEEN BLESSED with two great boys since our wedding day at the Sacred Heart Church. Our first son Ryen arrived in April 2012 while Jack was born in March 2015. I have to say, it was a surreal experience to be able to be there for their births. Both were life-changing moments for me, but I also really enjoyed them... even though Caroline probably didn't! Being there and watching something that I helped create coming into the world is something that will stay with me until my dying day.

I can only imagine how difficult it must have been for expectant parents during the Covid-19 pandemic with the restrictions placed on visitors, not to mention the difficulty in allowing the father in for the birth. Seeing your child come into the world changes your whole perspective on life.

For the first time, I felt like I had real responsibility. It's something that forces you to grow up fast. Suddenly you have people relying on you, so there has to be a routine and the last-minute plans or weekend visits to Bozo's Nite Club become a thing of the past.

If I'm totally honest, I'm a little relieved we have two boys as well. I don't know what I'd be like if they were girls and we had lads calling to the house or anything like that. That could go either way – I still have a gun!

But as long as they're healthy that's the main thing of course. They are great kids, and it has been good to see them starting to play football. Ryen was playing soccer with St John's Athletic in Lecarrow before Covid hit, as well as football with Roscommon Gaels. We're lucky that both St John's and the Gaels have good facilities and that he can play all year round. His friends are there too and that's really important. Ryen joined up with Roscommon Town closer to home last year.

They might be still young but both lads are showing signs of talent. It's something I won't be forcing on them though. I'm very conscious of the fact that just because I loved playing football and dedicated my adult life to it, doesn't mean that my sons will too. It took a lot of commitment and a little bit of selfishness to have the kind of career I had, but if that's what my lads want then they will have our full support.

I do try to encourage them to play as many sports as they can though and to enjoy themselves while taking part. I could never force them to like soccer or Gaelic football, I'd much rather they found their own way. Once they're playing some sort of sport or taking part in physical activity then I'm happy.

JACK WOULD BE completely unaware of my time playing Gaelic football and Ryen doesn't ask about it. He's a bit young to remember and he has his own heroes in this current Roscommon team.

He would have been to a lot of the games back then though and it's great to have some nice photographs with both of them after matches. Maybe they'll be impressed with it all someday, but for now Daddy definitely plays second fiddle to the present-day soccer and Gaelic football players.

Ryen is a lot like me, and at the moment he prefers soccer. It's good that both of them are also into Gaelic football though because they wouldn't get very far in Roscommon if they weren't! Whether they make it to underage development panels or anything like that isn't what's important at this stage.

I'm more focused on teaching them to kick properly off both feet and hand pass off both hands. That should be the main focus with lads that age so that they don't have to be coached to do the basics at the age of 14 or 15… or even at senior level for that matter. It's something I've been doing with the Roscommon Gaels nursery in the last couple of years, getting them comfortable on both sides so that they are confident in receiving and using the ball.

Another former Roscommon footballer Ciaran Henehan was running the academy before lockdown and he had it very well organised. The Gaels are lucky to have him and hopefully if he sticks with the club they can reap the benefits in years to come, much like St Brigid's did with their underage set-up.

« CHAPTER 17 »

ANTHONY CUNNINGHAM ANNOUNCED his departure from St Brigid's in 2008, after we failed to win our fourth county title in-a-row. Anthony had continued the good work done by Ger Dowd and won back-to-back Roscommon titles in 2006 and '07.

He had also taken us to the next level over those three years, winning a Connacht title in 2006 and helping us to believe that we could challenge regularly. He wasn't out of the game for long and ended up taking the Garrycastle hotseat, just down the road in Athlone ahead of the 2009 season.

For St Brigid's, it would be two years before we got back to the top of Roscommon football, and three years before we crossed paths with the talented Galwayman again.

We came out of a couple of barren years and regained the Fahey Cup in 2010 by beating Elphin by five points in the final. Noel O'Brien was in charge of us at this stage and there was plenty of optimism around the place once again.

Our experience was probably the difference that year. It was Elphin's first final in 24 years, and I think it's fair to say nerves played a part for them. Elphin were no pushovers and they had ended Castlerea St Kevin's' hopes of three titles in-a-row by dumping them out in the semi-finals. They just lacked that killer instinct and allowed us to come into the match. I was accurate from the dead-ball, converting six frees and a '45'. You'd never take winning county titles for granted, especially after watching Castlerea St Kevin's winning back-to-back championships in 2008 and '09, but there was a growing feeling around the club that we wouldn't have to wait too long for our next title.

WE WERE BACK on top in Connacht that year too. We hammered Eastern Harps in the quarter-finals before coming through a much trickier semi-final against Glencar-Manorhamilton. The Leitrim side even managed to put three goals past us up in Carrick. The final against Killererin in Tuam was the hardest game of the lot, and it took extra-time to separate us. We had a rake of different scorers that day – Senan Kilbride and Cathal McHugh grabbed our goals as we finally crossed the line with seven points to spare.

I was handed an unexpected promotion that year too when our captain Niall Grehan broke his ankle during training just before Christmas. Garvan was vice-captain and he was expected to take over and lead the side out for the remainder of the campaign. However, just ahead of our All-Ireland semi-final against Nemo Rangers, our manager Noel O'Brien took me aside.

'Garvan doesn't want to be captain,' he told me.

'But he's the vice-captain, why wouldn't he want to lead us out?'

'We've spoken to him… he just doesn't want to do it. Will you be captain?'

It was an honour to be asked but I felt I had to speak with Garvan before accepting just to make sure he was okay with me taking his place.

He said he was fine with it and that he turned down the captaincy because he didn't feel like he was one for making speeches or giving rallying calls in the dressing-room. He preferred to just concentrate on his own game and lead by example. As long as Garvan did his talking on the field, that was good enough.

We were fortunate to have lads like him all over the dressing-room, those who didn't need the captaincy in order to provide leadership. I felt so sorry for Niall, getting that injury and missing two massive games in our club's history (against Nemo Rangers and Crossmaglen). He was an outstanding player, and a man who drove the standards in our dressing-room to new heights.

There is a photo taken after the Nemo win, of myself and Niall, and it is one of my favourite photos. To see the happiness on his face after we had won shows what a real leader he was in every possible way.

I was still delighted to take over from Niall for the remainder of the All-Ireland series and the captaincy is something that I really enjoyed. It was a privilege to lead those men out onto the pitch and it motivated me to raise my game too.

The change in captaincy didn't disrupt our preparations for our stunning win over Nemo Rangers in the All-Ireland. Nemo are of the most decorated clubs in the history of the All-Ireland Club Championship and were heavy favourites to advance that day. All three of the Dolan brothers scored points, but it was Senan Kilbride who stood out with six. I was operating from deep, winning ball and setting up scores. I had plenty of space to operate in after Nemo midfielder David Niblock was sent off early in the second-half. There's no doubt that helped us, and we managed to grind out a two-point win.

Noel O'Brien was delighted afterwards and so too were our supporters and everyone involved with the club. It was the first time a Roscommon club had reached the All-Ireland club final since the days of the great Clann na nGael teams. The excitement in the weeks leading up to St Patrick's Day that year was something else. It didn't matter that we would come face to face with the dominant Crossmaglen Rangers from Armagh.

I HAVE ONLY ever managed to watch that final against the Ulster champions back on two occasions since 2011. To this day I'm still mad as hell with myself for how I underperformed. Noel had me deployed in a free role around midfield and it was something that had worked well against Nemo. Get free… get on the ball… and make things happen. It sounded simple in theory, but I felt I could have done with more guidance from the sideline.

The plan was for me to act as the playmaker, finding space between the lines and providing quick ball to the likes of Senan Kilbride and Cathal McHugh.

But it just didn't come off.

Instead of rushing in to close me down and leaving a hole for McHugh and Kilbride to run into, my opposite number just retreated in front of his full-back line and choked the space. His teammates were left with the simple task of mopping up breaking ball.

Our management team probably should have intervened earlier when it became clear our game-plan wasn't working. Or maybe I should have had the cop on to alter my approach. On big days like that you can get wrapped up in the occasion and you can lose the ability to think clearly.

I suppose that's where my own experience comes into it too and I should have acted when I realised the game was passing me by. I wasn't the only one having an off day and it didn't help that we managed to concede a couple of sloppy goals to a team that were hard enough to beat without any help. Crossmaglen were ruthless once they got their noses in front.

OF ALL THE games I've ever played, that one ranks as the most disappointing. We genuinely believed we were in with a good chance of winning the All-Ireland that year, and even though Cross were one of the best club sides to every come out of Ulster, we had no fear of them. To get that close and not play to our potential was something that took us all a long time to get over. There was never any guarantee that we would reach an All-Ireland final again.

I don't remember much of what happened at the full-time whistle.

I was in a daze, absolutely gutted.

I've also done my best to blank it out to be honest. As disappointed as I was though I had accepted the captaincy and I knew I couldn't go missing. You have to put personal disappointment aside and lead your teammates from the front. I did walk around the pitch congratulating the Cross players.

I despise losing at the best of the times and that was a bitter pill to swallow.

When the final whistle went there was bit of a lump in my throat, but at the time I thought I had done well to hide my heartbreak in front of the hard men from south Armagh. There's a picture of me leaning against a wall at the side of the pitch and Caroline and other family members are consoling me. She's wiping tears from my eyes.

I hadn't even realised I was crying. That Crossmaglen team would go on to win back-to-back titles the following year. We would get a shot at gaining some revenge in 2013 but we weren't to know that in '11.

BOTH TEAMS USUALLY go for a meal in the restaurant upstairs in Croke Park after the club final. It's not something either team really enjoys but it's much harder when you're on the losing side. Still, a good meal after a hard-fought game is always welcome and we thought it would line the stomach for the journey back to Roscommon at least. We were wrong.

We would have been better off stopping for Supermac's on the way home. As if losing an All-Ireland final wasn't bad enough, they fed us pasta and chicken you wouldn't give to the dog. To be fair, we were more interested in the pints of porter at that stage anyway. What I remember most is the lack of interaction with the Crossmaglen lads. Not that there was ever much craic out of them anyway. We respected them but there was also a certain level of disdain for them too, especially after that game. The feeling was mutual, and I don't think they lost too much sleep over us lads down south anyway.

I sometimes got the sense on the pitch that some of them had a real chip on their shoulders. Some of the 'sledging' was dreadful stuff, but I suppose it went both ways. Cross would do their level best to bully the opposition, and they didn't contain themselves to the players either, everyone got it… even innocent members of the backroom.

BETWEEN 2010 AND '13, it felt as though the seasons were just rolling into one. After our heart-breaking defeat to Crossmaglen, it wasn't long before we were back in action in the Roscommon championship. By now, we were head and shoulders above every other club in the county and our focus was on winning the bigger prizes.

The toughest obstacle we faced in Roscommon at that stage was complacency, and there were times when we almost came unstuck. As boring as it sounds, we had to learn to take one game at a time if we wanted to have a go at Connacht and the rest of Ireland. That year we were comfortable enough in the county championship and had another straightforward win over Elphin in the final. It's not being arrogant to say that we had to leave the county in order to be tested. We continued to play challenge matches against clubs from across Ireland so that we wouldn't be caught cold in the Connacht and All-Ireland series. That was something that worried us a little bit.

Those worries were justified in the opening stages of the Connacht semi-final against the Sligo champions Tourlestrane at Markievicz Park. They were four points up in no time and even though we slowly got into the game, they were still leading by a point at half-time.

Senan Kilbride was in great form that year and he scored six points in Sligo. I was going well in the playmaker role and managed to chip in with four points myself. We got a bit of luck too when Brian Egan was sent off for Tourlestrane, but we always felt we had an extra gear if needed and ended up winning by six points in the end.

On paper, we had been given the easier of the semi-finals and the winners of the other semi-final would prove to be our biggest test of the year so far. Corofin beat the Mayo champions Ballintubber in that one and our match was fixed for Kiltoom.

Defending Connacht champions and with home advantage, we were quietly confident of retaining our provincial title that year. No one told the Galway champions this though and they nearly ended our reign that afternoon.

Corofin were the hungrier side in the first-half and threw everything they had at us. I ended the day with six points, but I wasn't having it all my own way against Alan Burke. Senan and McHugh were getting it hard enough too and we just couldn't get our usual free-flowing game going.

The Mayo referee Liam Devenney came to our aid at times too. He gave nearly everyone in Kiltoom a yellow card and ruled out a Mike Farragher goal too. It looked soft but we said nothing.

The Corofin lads were understandably unhappy at the full-time whistle – Shane Curran of all people had to help escort Devenney and his officials back to the dressing-room. It was ugly stuff, but we've had plenty of days like that too I suppose. We had retained our Connacht title and that was all that mattered to us.

It had all gone to plan up to that point, but our preparations for the All-Ireland series were severely hampered when Noel O'Brien fell ill. Noel had done a remarkable job in guiding us to back-to-back Connacht titles and we felt we were banging on the door when it came to winning ours, and the county's, first All-Ireland club title too.

To help Noel with the running of the team, the club brought in Sean Kilbride, Marty McDermott and Peter McHugh. Suddenly there were a lot of new voices around the panel and the cohesion we had for the previous two years just wasn't there. It became a bit overcomplicated.

It was around this time that the club brought in a sports psychologist to help us take that final step. Our new 'football shrink' was Sligo woman Caroline Currid, who had just been a part of the Tipperary and Dublin All-Ireland winning backroom teams of the previous two years. She had a growing reputation and had also been part of Mickey Harte's backroom team in 2008 when Tyrone were champions.

We were told that Caroline had a Masters in sports psychology and that she had worked with the Kenyan runner David Rudisha at the London Olympics in 2012.

The whole concept of sports psychology was still a relatively new phenomenon back then, certainly for a bunch of Gaelic footballers from Kiltoom anyway. It took us some time to accept it as an important part of our preparation.

To be fair, even Paul O'Connell, who worked with Caroline right up until his retirement, took a while to get on board with the idea.

Caroline was impressive and has since gone on to enjoy even more success with All-Ireland winning teams, but at that time there were just too many chiefs trying to make themselves heard.

One incident stands out.

We were called to a meeting at the Hodson Bay Hotel prior to the All-Ireland semi-final against Garrycastle. It was huge match against a team just 10 miles down the road so everyone in the parish was talking about it. There were bragging rights up for grabs in Athlone and, of course, the Dolan boys had the added element of coming up against our cousins. It was real pressure cooker stuff.

The main points of the talk were how we should say nothing to the media in the build-up to the game and maintain discipline at all times on the pitch. Simple... don't speak to the local press... don't be giving silly frees away... and no stupid yellow cards. That was fine. We all agreed that keeping our heads would give us a better chance of winning.

Our problem wasn't with the message itself; it was the way it was drummed into us in the days and weeks before the game. We felt like lambs being sent to a slaughter.

Caroline was simply relaying a message from the management team, but the message sounded a bit like fear and paranoia. Stupid stuff like blanking the media so as not to give our opponents the edge.

You'd swear the Westmeath papers were doing a bit of spying for Anthony Cunningham on the side. Maybe they were, but we were hardly going to sit down with them and tell them all about our tactics or match-ups.

I think those messages we received caused fear and anxiety among some players in the camp and that made it much harder for lads to perform to their highest level. Rather than going in as a team who had reached the All-Ireland final the year before, we felt we were going in as underdogs, so it was advantage

Garrycastle even before throw-in.

Our neighbours in Athlone received another boost just before the match too when it came to the jerseys. Both clubs played in green and red, so one side would have to wear a change of strip for that semi-final. Garrycastle won that battle too.

Now that might seem like a small thing, but it was another psychological edge. They were permitted to wear their change strip, which was quite similar to their regular one. We, on the other hand, were forced to dip into the club's lost and found box for these yellow jerseys we'd never worn before.

Believe it or not, former players still talk about that incident and just like Manchester United's infamous grey kit of the 90s, those strips were put back in the lost and found box at the full-time whistle... never to be found again.

THE CONSTANT WARNINGS to keep our heads and avoid yellow cards really sapped some of the aggression from our play too. Garrycastle didn't have that problem and Cunningham had them fired up from the throw-in. They were playing on the edge, like you would expect in a big local derby, getting right into our faces and winning first and second ball. Not even referee Joe McQuillan's constant whistling could slow them down.

I still remember how tough it was out there.

There were less than two minutes on the clock, and I had the ball near the sideline looking for options... BANG!

I didn't even see my cousin James Dolan coming.

Suddenly the ball was stripped from my hands and there were Garrycastle players flooding forward from all angles. Things didn't really improve for me in that first-half but Cathal McHugh, Karol Mannion and Senan Kilbride kept the scoreboard ticking over and we somehow led by two at the break.

Despite our narrow lead, it was panic stations in the dressing-room at half-time. Robbie Kelly was picking up my cousin Dessie in the first-half, but Dessie was running riot. He was just unplayable. Robbie stood up during the break and pleaded with the management to switch him, but they failed to act.

Robbie would be back on Dessie again in the second-half before being replaced with John Murray after 10 minutes. Garrycastle were well on top by that stage though and it would take us 17 minutes to register our first score.

Our poor start after the break allowed Dessie and Co. to build up a lead of four points midway through the half. We were still in the game at that point and we were given a huge lift when David O'Shaughnessy was sent off.

We controlled possession from then on, but our luck had abandoned us. Ian Kilbride had a shot which was touched on to the post by the Garrycastle goalkeeper Cathal Mullin. Our afternoon ended with the referee giving Dessie a tap-over free after he blew our 'keeper for picking the ball up off the ground. It was hard on us but Garrycastle managed to hold on as we went looking for a goal in injury-time.

IT WAS THE only time we faced Garrycastle in a competitive fixture during my time with St Brigid's and it still hurts that we never really got going that day. The Athlone cousins still get a kick out of bringing that one up from time to time. The record books will always show that our neighbours dumped us out of the All-Ireland championship that year. It doesn't matter what happened afterwards.

I can look back and laugh about it now with Dessie, Gary and my other cousins, James Dolan and Alan Fox, who also played that day, whenever we meet up at weddings or family gatherings. In fairness to Dessie, he wouldn't be one for bringing it up anyway, it's usually the other cousins who'd make the most of the slagging.

The rivalry was put aside soon after the game, and St Brigid's as a club really got behind Garrycastle and offered whatever help was needed as they went on to face Crossmaglen in the final. Cunningham's men should probably have beaten them in the first game too but let them off the hook and were then well beaten in the replay. Those men from south Armagh were beginning to look invincible to some people.

THERE WAS A lot of talk and speculation back then that our defeat to Garrycastle might be the end of that St Brigid's team because the disappointment had followed the All-Ireland final agony from the year before. Even people within the club had started to ask questions. Had this team gone as far as it could?

Was an All-Ireland simply a step too far? There was also quite a bit of soul searching done in that dressing-room in Pearse Park in Longford.

It wasn't the first time people inside and outside the club had started to doubt us either. Even though we won back-to-back Connacht titles in 2010 and '11, we had also tasted defeat in 2005 and lost those two big All-Ireland games too.

It didn't really feel like it at the time, but all that pain would help bring us together and make us stronger for one final attempt at the summit the following year.

Though thoughts of glory in Croke Park and marching up the steps of the Hogan Stand could not have been further from our minds in that cold dressing-room in Pearse Park in 2012. We were a broken team and there was a black cloud hanging over the parish for a few weeks afterwards.

ON A PERSONAL LEVEL, I received some recognition for my performances in 2010 and '11, and I was honoured to receive the AIB award for best player in Connacht for both years. I also won the People's Choice award in 2010 to give me a double that year.

Following our 2012 All-Ireland club semi-final against Garrycastle, it was announced that myself and Dessie had won the provincial awards, the first time in the history of the award that two close relations had done so.

Jamie Clarke was the best player in Ulster and Colm 'Gooch' Cooper won the Munster award.

The awards ceremony in Dublin was a great example of how dangerous it can be when awards are given out to two family members at the same time.

When it came to pick an overall winner of the Club Player of the Year, they called out my name. I was mortified and knew straight away they had meant the Dolan sitting behind me. I went up to collect the award anyway, as Dessie was forced to sit there and clap. I even thought about making a speech to really rub it in.

The organisers came to me later and explained that there had been a mix-up.

Maybe I should have protested a bit more, but I suppose it was only fair to let Dessie have it since Garrycastle had just beaten us a few weeks before.

Individual awards are always nice but individual glory is not the reason I always strived to be the best player on the pitch. I just wanted to help the team and I knew that if I was winning the Man of the Match awards – which I did in seven out of 10 county finals – then it would go a long way in helping us over the line.

« CHAPTER 18 »

AFTER LEADING US to back-to-back Roscommon and Connacht titles, Noel O'Brien stepped down from his role as manager of St Brigid's shortly after our defeat to Garrycastle. Noel had helped guide us to the next level where we had become a match for anyone in Connacht and even further afield.

By the time he left, we believed we were among the top club sides in the country. He left big shoes to fill too, but he felt he had taken us as far as he could. There was also his own health to consider and I know that the last year was tough at times for him.

NOEL WAS NOW gone, and our two heart-breaking All-Ireland defeats were still fresh in our minds. It was a bleak dressing- room new manager Kevin McStay stepped into, just two days after the drawn All-Ireland club final between Crossmaglen and Garrycastle.

We were still feeling sorry for ourselves after the Garrycastle defeat, but Kevin made it clear from the start that we needed to move on quickly if we wanted to set the record straight. The former Mayo star brought Liam McHale and Benny O'Brien in with him as part of an impressive management ticket.

McHale had also won an All Star with Mayo and had been a top-class basketball player. Benny had played with Brigid's of course, helping to end that 28-year wait for a senior title in 1997, and would go on to successfully manage the club himself.

There was no doubt who the boss was from the first meeting though. Kevin had built up a reputation as someone who knew what he was talking about, and wasn't afraid to say it. Not only had he been a star of the Mayo team in the 80s and 90s, but he had also won a county title as manager of Roscommon Gaels in 1994 and impressed RTÉ viewers in his role as a co-commentator and pundit. Footballer, coach, pundit… Kevin was the complete package.

THE MESSAGE FROM our new management team was fairly straightforward from the beginning. We would have to toughen up and there would be no room for ego in the St Brigid's' dressing-room. The trio had a policy which was like that of the New Zealand All Blacks or Jim Gavin's great Dublin teams, there would be no place for those not willing to put the collective ahead of themselves.

Working hard, both as an individual and as a team, was a given. Kevin would speak about being honest in our efforts… the difference, he insisted, between a good team and a great one.

We knew we had to get back up on the horse after 2011 and '12. It was either go again or give it up altogether. I was hitting my mid-thirties at this stage but even I felt too young to just throw in the towel. Playing football was what we loved doing but we also knew we were running out of time.

The arrival of a new management team with fresh ideas gave us a desperately needed lift. It was like a fresh breeze blowing through the club and we all got taken along on it.

For Kevin, well, it didn't take him too long to realise that he was after walking into the dream scenario for a senior club manager in Roscommon. It was clear from the start that he would be managing a terrific group of players not too far from his own house.

He has since said how surprised he was by the level of skill on show at training. He had stumbled upon a panel of players who had been coached the right way from underage and were now comfortable with the basic skills of the game. I'm not sure whether that said more about the coaching at St Brigid's or the standard of Gaelic footballers elsewhere.

We were also fully committed to the cause. There was no way Kevin would have to go chasing lads or waste time texting and calling them for training. There was an established core group there by the time he arrived, and we drove everyone else on. We were hell-bent on getting over that final hump.

Our experiences over the previous few years had also made us a very tight-knit group, and Kevin, Liam and Benny tapped into that and helped us to all pull together in the one direction.

The team also had one more trump card over many others... hunger.

Despite our dominance in the Roscommon championship and our Connacht title wins, we still had a huge desire to go on and win even more silverware. We were entirely self-motivated and we drove each other on in training and when the chips were down in matches.

Our record in the Roscommon Senior Championship that year was immaculate, although we were given a bit of a scare when we faced St Faithleach's in the second round of matches.

We had comfortably beaten Kilbride on the opening weekend by 14 points. It was too easy for us and it probably led to some complacency in the build-up to the Faithleach's game.

Faithleach's had the three Murtagh brothers Ciaráin, Diarmuid and Brian playing for them. They were dangerous going forward but there was a belief that they had a soft centre and could be dominated around midfield.

And so that's how it went for most of the game. We cruised into the closing stages, fully confident that we were about the make it two wins from two. Then Kevin made some changes.

There was some confusion when our Man of the Match Damien Kelleher was called ashore. *What's he doing? We're nearly there!*

Faithleach's suddenly came alive and ran riot in the last quarter of the game, outscoring us by 1-5 to 0-1. We were lucky to escape from Ballyleague with our lives. We beat them by three points in the end, but it should have been far more comfortable than that.

They had us hanging on in the end, all because lads needed a run out.

I HAD MISSED the opening game against Kilbride but made my first championship appearance as a half-time substitute against Faithleach's. Maybe I was part of our second-half problem.

We improved in our third game with a 10-point win over Roscommon Gaels in Johnstown. I scored five points that day to open my account. It had been left to Senan Kilbride to shoulder much of the responsibility for scores up to then. Not that it fazed him.

Senan scored a goal and four points against Kilbride, a goal and three against St Faithleach's, and a goal and four against Roscommon Gaels. No wonder I was starting to feel old!

WE WERE DRAWN against Western Gaels in the quarter-finals. A niggly rivalry had developed over the previous few years between us, and I remember there was quite a bit of tension in the build-up. Some neutrals believed the Gaels would really test us and that there might even be a shock on the cards.

Unfortunately for both Western Gaels and the neutrals, the game was a real let-down. Neither side played flowing football and it turned very scrappy at times. I certainly played my part in that.

There were about 40 minutes gone on the clock when I tangled with Ultan Mulleady. He had been dragging and pulling out of me all afternoon. He had a hold of my jersey, so I threw an elbow back at him and he hit the deck.

It was a silly red card, but I still think it was worth it. I could never stand lads who were just sent out to annoy the opposition. It usually meant that their manager wasn't confident enough in their own ability.

I was forced to spend the last 20 minutes in the stand, watching on as the Gaels chipped away at our six-point half-time lead. Like our supporters, I was growing more nervous the longer the game went on. I could already see the headlines if we lost!

It was a good job Senan was unplayable that summer and his goal and six points kept our noses in front. Karol Mannion's performance further forward was also crucial as we set up our semi-final against Elphin. There was no one more relieved than me.

THAT ELPHIN SIDE had plenty of promise and we expected a tough game. They had appeared in the previous two county finals and there was a belief in some quarters that their time had finally come. My suspension fed into that belief and the game was hyped once again in the local media as a potential shock.

By this stage, we had seriously started to motor though, and we were quietly confident that we would stand up to whatever Elphin had to throw at us. We weren't confident for nothing. In the past three years we had battled the likes of Corofin, Crossmaglen and Garrycastle and had all grown because of it. With or without me, I was sure my teammates would give us all another day out at the Hyde.

They didn't let me down either. Gearoid Cunniffe played brilliantly as the link man between defence and attack, while Conor McHugh chipped in with a goal and a point. But, once again, it was that man Senan Kilbride who really stood head and shoulders above everyone else on the pitch. He helped himself to a goal and five points in one of the most one-sided semi-finals I've seen in Roscommon.

Elphin scored just five points as we sent out a clear message to the rest of the county that we hadn't gone away.

Completing a three in-a-row of county titles is a major feat but to go and do it twice in just a few years was something else. We were confident that we could achieve it and go on and do more damage in Connacht.

The final was a different story to our semi-final against Elphin and we made very heavy work of completing our second hat-trick of titles. Pádraig Pearses came to Kiltoom for that match and gave us a real scare in the second-half.

Just like the Faithleach's game in the group stage, we were in cruise control heading into the final quarter. I had already scored one goal and would end up with another one as well as three points from play, but Pearses went on a run towards the end. Our six-point advantage had been whittled down to two and the men from Woodmount had all the momentum.

It could have been all over that day, if at the end of normal time Peter Domican hadn't cleared Niall Carty's shot off the line. There had been no sign of this Pearses whirlwind for most of the match, but suddenly we were in a real fight.

I grabbed my second goal of the game four minutes into stoppage time and there was a huge collective sigh of relief all around the ground. We had survived by the skin of our teeth, but we didn't care. All that mattered to us was that we were Roscommon champions again and back on the road in Connacht.

From my own point of view, I was delighted to be back after suspension and contributing to the team. It's hard when you're not involved in the matchday panel. It was the reason I had stepped away from Roscommon seven years previously, I didn't like feeling like a spare part. Most players don't.

I knew I wouldn't be playing in the semi-final against Elphin, but I still felt I had an important role to play in helping the lads to prepare. I drove them on in training and made sure my marker wasn't given an easy time of it. If you take it easy not only are you cheating yourself, but you're also cheating your teammates.

That year, Kevin, Liam and Benny made it clear that we would all need to play our part if the club was to get anywhere near the Andy Merrigan Cup on St Patrick's Day. There would be no room for passengers.

OUR PERFORMANCES IN Connacht that year showed that we meant business and our confidence grew with each game we played. We felt unstoppable and we swatted Melvin Gaels aside by 15 points in the preliminary round after Leitrim star Emlyn Mulligan skied a penalty over the bar in the first few minutes. Shane Curran's mind games before he took that kick contributed to the miss.

That wasn't to be Mulligan's only involvement that day – he outscored me by eight points to seven and it was his late tackle that forced me off injured at half-time!

We met Salthill/Knocknacarra in the semi-final. We were a completely different team now, but I still had flashbacks to that day in 2005 when they had annihilated us in the Connacht final. It was hard to believe that seven years before we were sitting in that dressing-room in Salthill wondering if we would ever reach their level, and now here we were.

That game showed the evolution of the St Brigid's team between 2005 and '12. Just six of the team that had been taught a footballing lesson in our first-ever Connacht final remained. Karol Mannion and Ian Kilbride were two of the survivors from 2005 and they were immense against Salthill seven years on.

We were fitter and stronger this time around, too, and we had been conditioned to hunt in packs. We turned the ball over time after time and even though they threatened a comeback in the closing stages, we just had too much for them.

Seven points was the gap in the end, a point for each of those years we had been building up to this moment.

We were cruising through the province, but there was no fear of us getting complacent. Our training sessions were as intense as ever because lads knew something special was happening and wanted to be part of it on match days.

There aren't too many Roscommon sides who can say they've beaten Galway opposition in Salthill and then gone on to beat a Mayo side in a Connacht final in Castlebar, but that's exactly what we did in 2012.

Ballaghaderreen were our opponents, and it was seen as an 'all-Roscommon' final for obvious reasons… though there might be a few Mayo folk who wouldn't agree. Just like our All-Ireland semi-final against Garrycastle earlier in the year, there was plenty of talk of bragging rights in the build-up, and the opening 20 minutes or so were cagey.

Ballaghaderreen were a good side and they made life difficult for us, running back to form a blanket of 12 and 13 bodies every time we had possession.

At half-time, we were leading a low-scoring game, six points to five. Our own Mayomen still weren't happy though and Liam McHale took aim at Karol Mannion.

'Are you hitting your highest levels? I don't think you are…. it's not good enough. Get your finger out or you'll be coming off.'

It was clever man management.

McHale knew Mango could take it and would raise his game for the second-half. It also had the desired effect for the rest of the dressing-room. You could nearly hear lads thinking… *Karol Mannion? Hooked in a major final?*

Jesus, what must they think of me!

It was the kick up the arse we all needed.

We got a stranglehold of the game after the interval and there were good performances all over the pitch. Senan was on fire once again, hitting a goal and five, while Richie Blaine was also impressive. I chipped in with three points and we looked comfortable in the end.

THREE CONNACHT TITLES on the spin was a fantastic achievement but we weren't finished there. Most of us could remember the Clann teams of the 80s and their dominance of Roscommon and Connacht. Clann won six provincial titles in-a-row from 1984 to '89 and appeared in four successive All-Ireland finals between 1987 and '90, losing them all. Roscommon Gaels had also reached an All-Ireland final in 1976, only to be hammered by a great St Vincent's side from Dublin.

For those of us who lived in south Roscommon and followed that great Clann team of the 80s around Connacht, their success was etched into our memories. But I also remembered watching my hero Tony McManus dominate teams in

Roscommon and Connacht and then fall short when it came to the big one. That was something I was desperate to avoid at all costs.

In a way, I used Clann's lost finals to motivate myself and I'm sure there were a few others who did the same. It helped to focus my mind on how hard I'd have to push myself if I wanted to avoid a repeat of the previous two years.

Did we want to be remembered as a good team that got to All-Ireland finals, or remembered as a great team and the first Roscommon side to bring one home?

This question echoed in my mind as we trudged around Kiltoom for the rest of the winter, including during our morning session on St Stephen's Day.

What is the point in getting this far only to fail again?

We had faced the best teams in Ireland from 2010 to '12 and deep down we all knew there was nothing to fear.

That session on the morning of St Stephen's Day was one of the best sessions we ever had – the intensity and pace, and overall quality of everything we did that morning, was so enjoyable. We meant business. Liam's sessions were always enjoyable, but this one was savage. Lads were hammering one another.

« CHAPTER 19 »

A STORM WAS brewing at Hodson Bay in early 2013 and it was threatening to blow our All-Ireland campaign off course.

It started when a couple of the county boys mentioned that they wanted to take part in the FBD League that year for Roscommon. They were enjoying playing under John Evans, I think, and worried about losing their place in the team for the league and championship later in the year.

We had a meeting at the hotel. Representing the players were myself and Niall Grehan. The management team was there too, along with our Roscommon contingent, Karol Mannion and Ian and Senan Kilbride. The boys wanted to go back playing with the county and Kevin McStay was on the fence about it. I wasn't.

'Lads, if ye go back playing that FBD shite… I'm packing it in,' I told them. A bit dramatic maybe.

Karol Mannion could be stubborn at times but the three of them eventually agreed to hold off on the county until at least the National League.

Imagine disrupting a crack at the All-Ireland Club Championship just so you could play FBD! It wasn't like there was a trip to New York anymore for winning the FBD League!

OUR BATTLES WITH Crossmaglen in 2007 and '11 weren't for the faint-hearted, but things were to get even hairier in 2013 when we decided we had taken enough abuse from the Ulster champions and it was time we gave some back.

The management team wasn't aware of it, but the senior players on the panel let it be known that we weren't prepared to just stand there and take it in Mullingar that year. Cross had got into our heads at times during the previous two games and we couldn't allow them to do it again.

It was made clear to every man that we would have to stand up to them and be willing to play right on the edge, sometimes even crossing the line. There could be no repeat of what happened against Garrycastle the year before.

That All-Ireland semi-final was one of the most enjoyable I have ever played, in if I'm honest. Two good sides going hammer and tongs at each other for over an hour. It was pure mayhem really and I loved every minute of it.

It wasn't just confined to the field of play either. I remember a couple of incidents in the first-half when some of their supporters came out from behind the goal just to shout abuse at me. The umpires did their best to push them back through the wire before things got out of hand.

I had enough to be worrying about with the likes of the Kernans, never mind a handful of angry supporters from south Armagh! Oisin McConville went off injured in the first-half, which helped. I loved the physicality of it though and the feeling that after two heart-breaking defeats, we were finally gaining the upper hand on the men from Ulster. It was an arm-wrestle rather than a game of free-flowing football, but that was fine with us.

I was marking Paul Kernan that day and I had no problem using some of the 'dark arts' against him. It was something the Ulster teams had become the masters of, but by this stage other teams had copped onto it and were prepared to dish it out too. I gave Kernan all sorts of abuse that day.

Most of it was pure bullshit, but if it helped me to wind him up and throw him off his game then who cares?

We felt we had no choice but to get into their heads. They were going for their third All-Ireland title in-a-row and had most teams beaten before the ball was even thrown in. You had to win the mental battle with them if you wanted to have any chance of keeping up.

KEVIN AND HIS team were brilliant in the build-up to that game too and they deserve a lot of credit. We had blocked out all the hype and focused on the factors we could control. We knew that every little detail mattered, and our preparation was spot on.

One thing Kevin had noticed while watching the Ulster final was the way in which Cross tried to bully every member of the Kilcoo backroom team, even down to the water-boys. So around eight weeks before we were due to travel to Cusack Park, Kevin announced a couple of changes and he brought Basil Mannion and Tom Lennon in as runners.

Cross had their work cut out if they fancied bullying those two!

THE GAME ITSELF seemed to go by in a blur. I was drained by the end of it and it wasn't until I was being interviewed by Brian Carthy afterwards that I became aware of how significant the result was.

Cross didn't take being dethroned too well either and there may have been a few slaps thrown at Shane Curran. Come to think of it, he probably deserved them! He had played a big part in getting Kyle Carragher sent off just before the end.

Carragher had stuck out an arm, and Cake threw himself to the ground. The letter of the law would say it was a striking offence, but Cake was caught on camera looking out between his hands to see what the referee had given.

It was a case of giving Cross a taste of their own medicine and if that meant being a bit 'cute' then so be it.

We were tired of leaving Mullingar with our tails between our legs.

I was pleased with my own performance that day too. I scored a goal and two points and probably could have got a second goal if I hadn't been taken out as I went to pull the trigger. Conor McHugh was following up and he stuck it away instead. It didn't matter how it went in as long as we won.

I was relieved when the final whistle went even though I was enjoying myself. The result was the most important thing and there was a feeling among players, management and supporters that we had finally slayed the dragon and taken a massive step towards Roscommon's very first All-Ireland club title.

The only fear now was that we had peaked in the semi-final, believing that the hard work had already been done.

The job was still far from finished, and we would have to refocus before St Patrick's Day. It wasn't going to get any easier against a star-studded Ballymun Kickhams team which featured the likes of Philly McMahon, Dean Rock, James

McCarthy, John Small and Davy Byrne. Some of those men would go on to form the backbone of the most successful county team Gaelic football has ever seen.

BALLYMUN HAD COME through the ultra-competitive Dublin championship, so we knew it would be a huge test. We also knew they would be as physically tough as Crossmaglen and I worried whether lads' heads were right going into it. Beating a team like Crossmaglen can lead to complacency.

Was Mullingar an All-Ireland final for some of our boys?

To make things worse, I had broken my finger during training in the lead-up to the final. I was in a lot of pain and would have struggled to make it through the Ballymun game if not for our physiotherapist Pat Regan. Pat made a splint and a mould for the injured finger which reduced the mobility but allowed me to play. It wasn't ideal preparation, but I would sooner have had the finger cut off than miss out on the biggest game of my life.

When Pat wasn't making me splints and moulds for my damaged finger, he was busy dragging me to Mass in Ballybay Church on the day of the final!

St Patrick's Day that year fell on a Sunday and our match was down for a 3.45pm throw-in. The whole parish was on edge that day and none more so than Pat. He phoned me that morning to check on the hand and then ended up calling down to the house. Pat was more than just our physio.

He was at times our psychiatrist, confidante, guardian and a million other things too. He was a crucial part of the backroom and travelled all over the country with us.

'Come on Frankie… we'll go to Mass,' he said when he arrived at the door that day.

'Mass, Pat? Have you forgotten we have a match up in Dublin today?'

He wouldn't take no for an answer and so off we went to morning Mass. Every soul in the church that day must have been wondering what we were doing there when we slipped in the side door. We were due to be playing at Croke Park just a few hours later and here we were looking for divine inspiration!

FORMER DUBLIN FOOTBALLER Paul Curran, who would later go on to manage Clann na nGael, was over Ballymun at that stage – they had beaten Dr Crokes of Kerry in their semi-final. As much as we were looking forward to our second bite of the All-Ireland cherry, we knew it would be a massive battle.

It turned out to be a dreadful day for football. The ball felt like a bar of soap at times and lads were slipping and sliding all over the place. As bad as the conditions were, our slow start is still difficult to explain. We were creating chances, but Ballymun were clinical every single time they got into scoring range.

They were on a roll in the opening 10 minutes and wiping the floor with us. They led by 2-3 to 0-1 and our supporters were probably beginning to fear the worst. We were just trying to hang on until the half-time whistle.

It was a completely different game to the one against Crossmaglen. Our semi-final had been a slow, punishing brawl but this was real end-to-end stuff. The pace was unreal.

Just half-way through the first half and we were already desperate for a goal to give us some sort of lifeline. But as well as being dangerous in attack, Ballymun had gone through the Dublin championship without being breached once. They had even managed to put the shackles on the great 'Gooch' Cooper in the semi-final.

What they hadn't counted on were the performances of Senan Kilbride and Karol Mannion, who lit up a dark Croke Park that afternoon.

While we chipped away at their first-half lead, the north Dubliners were still dominating us around the middle of the park, and I remember Ronan Stack being sent out there to help put out fires. We were being overrun and it was obvious that we needed to get Garvan on for the second-half. His physicality would be crucial if we wanted to have any chance of competing.

WE WERE TAKING on water in that first-half and I was frantically searching the sideline for any activity or any sign that reinforcements were on their way. But Kevin was never one for changing things too early and he was clearly happy to let the starting 15 come up with their own solution.

It was a case of… 'You're the boys who got us into this mess… so now go and dig us out!' That's just how he operated but it was obvious we needed to change something or else Ballymun would continue to run all over us.

It had nothing to do with Garvan being my brother. He could have been anyone, but he had the attributes we needed that day to turn the game back in our favour. In fairness to Kevin, I could see why he would have been reluctant to bring Garvan on too early and see him pick up a yellow card.

He had taken him off during the semi-final for that very reason.

By the time the whistle went to end the half, we had somehow managed to claw our way back to within four points. It must have been a terrific game for the neutrals as Ballymun led by 2-6 to 1-5.

I sprinted back to the dressing-room and at the same time Kevin was making his way down from the stand where he had watched the first-half. Robbie Kelly had been injured just before Christmas, so Kevin had given him the responsibility of getting everyone settled and quiet in the dressing-room at half-time before the management gave their talk.

A solicitor by trade, the job suited Robbie!

I'm sure he was having second thoughts that day though when I burst into the dressing-room, the eyes bulging out of my head.

'Where's McHale?' I roared. No sign.

Into the treatment room then where our Mass-going physio Pat Regan was.

'Where's McHale?

'He's gone to the toilet'.

I stormed into the toilets, just as McHale was heading into one of the cubicles. There wasn't enough time to wait for him to come back out, so I squeezed in beside him and grabbed him around the collar.

He stood there looking down at me. 'Are you okay, Frankie?'

He could have given me a box!

'Look Liam, we're getting killed in midfield. Ye have to bring Garvan on before this gets away from us.'

He could see it too. He agreed a change would have to be made... but would it be okay if he used the toilet first? No worries Liam, you fire away.

Things were a bit frantic when I walked back into the dressing-room. So much for our resident solicitor calling order! It later transpired that Kevin had got lost in the maze of elevators on the way down from the stand. Some of the senior lads such as Karol and Mark O'Carroll had spoken well when the lads had first arrived in at the break, but now there was too much talking going on and we were in danger of going down a rabbit hole.

Kevin was in the management room with the other members of the backroom by this point and Mango had gone in to tell them they needed to speak to us, because there were too many people talking.

WHEN KEVIN AND Liam did arrive in, they rejigged things brilliantly. Garvan was brought on at midfield and Ian Kilbride was pushed back to centre-back. Suddenly there was far more physicality running through the spine of the team.

The real masterstroke though was moving Darragh Donnelly from centre-back right up to centre-forward. That changed the whole complexion of the game and we played like a completely different team in the second-half. The changes gave us more of an assurance about our play and we got on a lot more ball after the break.

We all lifted it a level too. A good indication of which team has the momentum is the breaking ball. We were much sharper to it in the second period and that allowed us to enjoy more control over the game.

Our full-back line was crucial in that second-half. The lads really got on top of Dean Rock and Ted Furman, and frustrated the hell out of them. Shane Curran in goals played a vital role in that too. He was constantly in the ear of any Ballymun player, official or supporter who would listen.

He homed in on Furman in particular though. The Ballymun forward had given Johnny Murray a real roasting in the first-half but Cake didn't let that deter him.

'Johnny's cleaning you out, Furman.

'You're just no good… are ya?

'Ye'll be winning nothing today!'

On and on it went for the next 30 minutes. Cake doesn't have to try too hard to get on people's nerves and his jibes certainly got to Furman that day.

Whether it was a tactical switch or whether he had just had enough of Cake, I don't know, but Ted ended up playing around the middle of the field as the game wore on.

Cake might come across as a bit of a lunatic at times but he's also an incredibly intelligent goalkeeper. I have taken my fair share of slagging and abuse in my time, but I wouldn't have enjoyed playing as a forward for Ballymun that day. The constant mouthing can put you off your game, even for just a split second.

The goalkeeper has an advantage too, in that he can stand there for their entire game throwing abuse at the opposition while organising his own players. I'm only surprised that more goalkeepers don't engage in a bit of psychological warfare from time to time. Or maybe they do, and it's just not picked up on.

Peter Domican, Ronan Stack and my brother Darren deserve a mention for their performances in that second-half too. They were brilliant in and out of possession, but every single player played a part. It was much better all round and, without wanting to sound cocky, I felt that we could have won it with a bit more to spare in the end.

The final few minutes were maybe a little bit more dramatic and nerve-racking then they needed to be, but winning was all that mattered.

WHILE I SCORED the winning point at the very end, it was Senan Kilbride's goal in the first-half that proved to be the real turning point. It would have been almost impossible to rescue the situation in the second-half without it. Both he and Karol Mannion were unbelievable that day and Mango got a very clever goal too where he followed up on an attack and fisted the ball low into the ground. Those boys were the definition of 'big game' players. Darren was outstanding also, playing probably his best game for the club. His kick-pass to Mango for Senan's goal was one of the best passes I've ever seen.

As for the clinching point at the very end, well, I can still feel the hairs stand up on the back of my neck to this day.

The tension was almost unbearable going into the closing stages. There was never more than a point in the difference and both sides were just waiting for the other team to blink. It really could have gone either way and neither side really deserved to lose it.

It came down to the very last possession in the game.

We had thrown away another easy chance and John Small took possession for Ballymun and raced down the wing… the Ballymun supporters roaring him on from the Cusack Stand. Those who have watched Dublin in recent years might find this next bit hard to believe, but John undercooked a hand pass and allowed Niall Grehan to get his hand in and tap it loose.

Niall then tore out in front of Jason Whelan to complete the turnover and set us on our way towards the Canal End.

I CAN STILL hear that wave of St Brigid's' noise ringing in my ears. It seemed to carry the ball up the pitch, where it met Garvan Dolan at full tilt. He just managed to get his hand pass away before being taken out.

I was left with two options… either go towards the ball and get clobbered for a free, just inside Ballymun's half… or trust that the ball would skid up off the surface and make it through to me.

Luckily, it bounced into my hands as I vaulted over Conor Weir, who had been a fingertip away from winning possession back for Ballymun.

Looking back at the video today, I did well to keep my balance, steady myself and squeeze a shot off with my left foot as Ballymun defenders swarmed in to smother me. Croker wasn't full by any means but the noise around the place when that one went over was deafening. You could almost hear the relief from the St Brigid's' supporters.

A surreal feeling.

The full-time whistle went shortly after that and it was pure mayhem. There were bodies sprawled all over the place. The dejected Ballymun lads fell to the turf exhausted, a pain we knew all too well. The adrenaline had kicked in for us this time around as we were mobbed by the substitutes and backroom team.

Apart from the win over Crossmaglen in the semi-final, it was probably the best feeling I've ever had after a game of football. Sheer ecstasy.

In the aftermath, my mind drifted back to all the hard winter training sessions in Athlone and Kiltoom, and the thousands of hours I had spent on those quiet evenings in the back garden. No amount of practice or visualisation could have prepared me for that feeling in Dublin, however. The week of the game, myself and Niall Grehan and Mark O'Carroll spent two hours on a wet miserable evening shooting and passing – some of those shots were identical to my last shot to win the game.

THERE HAD BEEN one moment towards the end of the game when it looked like we would come up short yet again.

We won a lineball over at the Hogan Stand with a minute or two to go and I was confident that I could strike it over the bar. It was a kick I had practiced many times while training at Croke Park and something I had done a few times in big games.

This time, however, things didn't go to plan.

My only excuse is that the ground was very heavy that day and my legs were nearly gone after almost an hour of frantic football. If I could have the moment again, I'd probably kick it short and try to work a better scoring position.

Cake had appeared out of nowhere too, just before I went to kick it. He decided to give the Ballymun lads a break from the abuse and sprinted the entire length of the pitch to give me some advice instead.

'I'll hit this one,' he said confidently… 'I'll kick it over'.

'You will in your hole. Get back in goal… you stupid b*****d!'

In hindsight, I should have let him take it. While his mouth must have been tired, his legs were far fresher than mine and there was no doubt he had the ability to get distance on it. But when you're a forward and you're playing with confidence you want to kick everything.

My attempt landed around the 13-metre line and Cake must have cursed me as he ran all the way back down to the Hill.

That All-Ireland final was a credit to both sets of players. The conditions were poor but that only added to the drama and the thrills and spills. Unlike the Crossmaglen game, and Cake's verbals aside, there wasn't a feeling of animosity between the sides.

We were both just intent on playing football. At the end, it was just sheer relief. When John Small advanced with the ball I feared the worst. Those were fine margins between winning and losing.

Looking back, I'm convinced that the noise from our supporters carried us down the field like a wave. The cheers when we won the turnover seemed to create momentum with each phase of the move, ending in a huge roar when the ball went over the bar.

I had never experienced anything like those few seconds between winning possession and slotting it over. It's something that I'll never forget for as long as I live. Being on the pitch that day with Garvan and Darren made it even more special.

IT MIGHT SEEM strange, but the celebrations felt slightly muted that day as we made our way up those 34 steps on the Hogan Stand. Maybe we really did feel we had done the hard work by finally getting the better of Crossmaglen in the semi-final. But I think it was because we knew how losing an All-Ireland final felt and didn't want to be rubbing Ballymun's noses in it.

You could see how much it meant to our loyal supporters though, particularly the older members of the club, who had had to watch our neighbours Clann na nGael dominate in Roscommon and Connacht for years. It was very emotional talking to them afterwards and I became a bit overwhelmed when it finally sunk in that we had delivered a title that no other Roscommon club had ever won.

There was no singing or shouting in the dressing-room as we got changed afterwards, the Andy Merrigan Cup sitting there beside us.

Kevin McStay came into the dressing-room and reminded us that we had to respect our opponents. Not that Ballymun would have heard us or anything, but we remained dignified anyway.

We huddled together in the warm-up room with the cup in the centre of our circle. McStay gathered us around him for one more talk before heading home.

'Now men, as a group you may never be here again. Some of you will stop playing altogether and there's no guarantee that the rest of you will scale this mountain again. Some of you won't even see each other again for a number of years, but I can tell you for sure that you'll be at each other's funerals… hopefully many years from now.'

Kevin was hammering home his point that we had reached the peak and there were no guarantees that we'd ever get to repeat a day like that again. It was his way of bringing home to us the scale of our achievement and warning us to soak up the moment. His words would turn out to be prophetic in the years after 2013, but it was hard to believe the only way was down at that moment in Croke Park.

One of my regrets from that day is that there were very few pictures taken in the dressing-room. Nowadays, lads have photos and videos uploaded to Instagram even before they've had a beer! It's a pity because it would have been nice to have more reminders of us all together after just winning the All-Ireland.

A few lads walked away soon after our greatest day and so it was the last time that group was all together.

After getting changed, we went along to the Croke Park restaurant for another round of that post-match chicken and pasta, though it was much easier to stomach this time around than it had been after our defeat to Crossmaglen in 2011. We all had one or two bottles of beer with the dinner too, but there was to be no alcohol on the bus back to Roscommon. That was down to Kevin McStay, who was conscious that there would be young supporters there to welcome us home later that night.

It was a very sober but happy bus journey back to Roscommon.

We disembarked on the bridge in Athlone and walked the cup back across the Roscommon border. It was a great feeling to share that moment with the supporters. Then it was back to the Hodson Bay Hotel for a celebration and that's when the real craic started!

Everyone associated with the club was there that night, and even some who weren't, including the well-known singer songwriter Phil Coulter. He was staying in the hotel for another engagement but that didn't stop Cake from dragging him in to perform for the new All-Ireland club champions.

AFTER A MEAL and a few pints in the Hodson Bay, it was back to the club to continue the celebrations. As I've said before, I always enjoy the days after a big win more. You're always drained immediately after the match and only too aware that some of the lads slapping your back and buying you pints had probably spent time slating you in the past. You can relax with your teammates the day after without having to humour people.

The texts usually went around on the Monday to arrange a team drinking session somewhere in Athlone, Galway or Dublin. That Monday after the All-Ireland was no different and we ended up at The Snug in Athlone.

The place was mobbed on account of it being a Bank Holiday and there were six of us who couldn't even get in the door. We decided to walk across the road to Seán's Bar where we could enjoy a few pints in comfort.

From what I remember, the floor in The Snug had to be replaced soon after that session too.

After doing our usual tour of the local schools later in the week, I ended up in Dublin with Cake and Cathal McHugh and a few others. I woke up one morning and one of the lads wanted to go for a 'curer'.

We managed to polish off two breakfasts each in Copper Face Jack's, where we stayed the previous night, before getting a taxi to Capel Street in search of an early house. I was standing outside after a few bottles and spotted Louis Copeland's shop. I had met Louis a couple of times, so decided to pop into him for a chat. It turned out to be the most expensive chat I've ever had, because I came out with a suit worth €1,200!

Caroline wasn't too impressed when she found the receipt and I think I only wore it once, to the club dinner dance that year.

THAT VISIT TO Capel Street might have been painful, but it was nothing compared to the pain I was experiencing in my neck and back since the final whistle at Croke Park. I had tried to ignore it at first, but it kept getting worse and now I was at the stage where I had to use the gear stick with my right hand.

I thought it would be wise to get it checked out as soon as everything calmed down and I was glad I did.

It turned out I had put a disc out in my neck and there was a trapped nerve beneath it. I had been in plenty of discomfort in the dressing-room after the match, but I put it down to a heavy fall and the lads jumping on me at the full-time whistle. I could barely lift my arms to dress myself and the pain hadn't got any better during the homecoming and celebrations back in Roscommon.

I went to see Gary O'Toole, the ex-swimmer in Dublin, and he advised me that I would need surgery to put it right. The operation option wasn't straightforward, so I went and got a second opinion from my cousin Keith Fox who is also a physiotherapist. Keith agreed with Gary's assessment, confirming that surgery was the only option if my neck hadn't corrected itself within the next few weeks. He told me to come back to him to arrange the operation if the pain hadn't gone away in two months and he gave me some exercises to do in the meantime.

I stuck at the exercises for the next few weeks even though I was in constant pain and then one day, around the seven-week mark, I woke up and the pain had suddenly disappeared. I couldn't believe it at first and I kept moving the neck and shoulder to make sure I wasn't imagining things.

I had been bracing myself for the surgery, but the disc must have got sick of hearing me complain about it and decided to head back in. It was a huge relief because the last thing a player in his mid-thirties wants is risky surgery, not to mention the impact weeks of rehabilitation would have on work.

A pain in the neck aside, the whole community was on a high for weeks after our big day at Croke Park, but we would have to come back down to earth at some point. It wasn't long before we were brought back to reality with a bang... in Kilmore of all places!

FOR ABOUT THREE years, our seasons seemed to run into each other. The All-Ireland club series would finish in March and we'd be back out for league fixtures very soon after that. It gave us little time to rest and reflect on what we had achieved. Motivation was also hard to come by for those league games, especially after you've just reached the 'Holy Grail' of club football.

It was only fitting then that we were beaten in our first league game back on a horrible pitch up in north Roscommon. We got some amount of stick afterwards too. Kevin McStay had warned us that being All-Ireland champions put a huge target on our backs and it was huge motivation for our opponents, and Kilmore certainly lapped it up!

To be fair, we had more of a team on the beer up in Dublin than what was available for selection that day, but there was no harm in keeping us humble.

From Croke Park to the muck of Kilmore. At least they looked after us at the full-time whistle, with a great spread of tea and sandwiches. They certainly enjoyed themselves anyway!

« CHAPTER 20 »

THE MOST NOTICEABLE change in Kiltoom following our All-Ireland club final was the fact that Kevin McStay was no longer our manager. Kevin had nothing left to prove with us, or any other club for that matter, and decided to walk away while we were still on a high.

I think Kevin could also see the writing on the wall, and knew that it was more difficult to build hunger and motivation after winning the biggest prize of all. Kevin, Liam McHale and Benny O'Brien had brought it all together the year before and if they stayed on, I think things could have been much different through the remainder of 2013.

From a selfish point of view, it was disappointing Kevin didn't sign on for just one more year. I know he had commitments with RTÉ and that he had nothing really left to prove, but it would have been nice to have a crack at winning back-to-back All-Irelands.

I would have loved to know what Kevin was thinking in the dressing-room after our win over Ballymun. He could obviously tell that a few of our lads would take a step back and that some of the older lads might step away completely. I was 35 and even though I was still in good shape, retirement did cross my mind on a couple of occasions, especially with the pain in my neck and back in the weeks after.

You start to think about whether you want the hassle of another year of training four and five nights a week, and constantly having to watch what you're eating. Did I want to skip pints and have to put myself though recovery sessions and injury rehabilitation? Part of me thought it was the right time to step away so that I could enjoy life more.

I just didn't bank on Karol Mannion leading an intervention!

Mango called me about a month after the All-Ireland club final to tell me that some of the lads were heading off to America for the summer and that we'd be struggling when they came back.

'F**k it, Mango… I'm thinking of packing it in myself!'

That was the last thing he wanted to hear and immediately started to talk me around. He was laying it on thick, guilt tripping me into sticking it out for one more year.

'This is the worst time to go Frankie. New manager coming in and all,' he said.

He was asking me if I wanted to be standing down in Kiltoom watching us getting hammered that summer. *Jesus Christ Mango, give me a break!*

His plea hit a nerve, of course, and when the slipped disc in my neck righted itself, I took it as a sign that I needed to stay on and help us defend our titles.

BENNY O'BRIEN WAS the man to step into the void left by Kevin McStay. Benny is a great fella, but it was always going to be a tough ask for anyone to fill Kevin's shoes, especially after the club had just had the best season in the history of Roscommon club football.

Benny was also quieter than Kevin and he didn't go as far into the finer details as the Mayoman had done. Liam McHale had also worked very well with Kevin and that dynamic had been crucial in helping us to reach the next level as a team. They had complemented each other brilliantly and, with all due respect to Benny, who did very well that year, that partnership was a major loss to the club.

I had played alongside Benny when we won the senior championship back in 1997. He was a fine footballer and I liked him a lot, but his appointment in 2013 was a surprise to me. He had been a selector the year before of course, but I assumed that if anyone was going to get the job after Kevin left, it would have been McHale. Liam did return as coach and we were glad to still have him in some capacity.

I liked and respected Kevin, don't get me wrong, but to me Liam was the main man behind the operation in 2013. I was also very close to him.

From the very first moment they walked into the Hodson Bay Hotel the previous March, Kevin and Liam had made it clear what they expected of us. They told us in no uncertain terms that they were there to manage, and we were there to play.

I looked around the room that night and for the first time I saw that every member of the panel was fully engrossed. We followed them from that moment on and they led us all the way to the top of those steps in the Hogan Stand.

WHILE THE CHANGE in management made headlines, other events behind the scenes would have a negative effect on the panel that year.

Just before the summer, a few of the younger lads, my brother Darren included, decided they were heading over to America to make a few handy dollars out there. Some of us more senior players felt we should all stick together for one more year to try and defend our title. But I suppose it's easy to say that when you're in your mid-thirties and have a wife and child at home.

Six of the lads, including five starters from the All-Ireland final, flew out to Boston that summer. Darren came home in July with all the war stories and he was followed by a few of the others. But Peter Domican was one of the six and he had decided to continue travelling after his time in Boston. Domo was a huge loss for us while the rest of the lads were hardly in championship shape after their summer of fun. That was something that would come back to haunt us later in the year.

WE WERE STILL the All-Ireland club champions heading into the spring and summer of 2013 of course. But it seemed that for some of the lads, winning it once was more than enough. There were still a few of us knocking around who thought we could go and repeat the achievement that year. We also knew that the window of opportunity was about to slam shut in our faces. It was now or never.

It was great to win one title but retaining it would have put us among the truly great clubs. I was one of the players who felt that 2013 was our last chance saloon because lads were getting on and the same quality didn't seem to be coming through to replace them.

In the end, Kevin McStay's post-match talk at Croke Park would become reality as players suddenly became unavailable for large chunks of the year and others just seemed to drop off the face of the Earth completely. I'm not joking, there was even talk locally of a black hole somewhere in south Roscommon that was swallowing some of our young players up.

AS MUCH AS I still wanted to play and make a difference, there comes a time for every footballer when you realise the end is getting near. The body isn't doing what it once did or you're not recovering as quickly as before. There are also other things going on too, like family and work commitments, and all the other stuff away from football. Your teammates seem to be getting younger each year as well and it's time to move on to let someone else through.

It's a hard thing to explain but it was like a feeling of loss, knowing that things will be different and that I wouldn't be sitting in the dressing-room listening to the slagging and bullshit each week. I got this feeling of dread when I realised the end of the road was near. There was a real fear of not being involved anymore. I dreaded walking away and tried my best to delay it as much as possible.

I didn't need much encouragement to stay on when Karol Mannion called me in April 2013, and I made up my mind quickly to throw everything I had into one more year with the club.

WE WERE STILL an impressive outfit at county level, and we wrapped up our fourth title in-a-row when we beat our old rivals Western Gaels in that year's final. There was even talk in some quarters at that time of us going on to match the great Clann team of the 80s and 90s, but some of us inside the camp knew better.

I was in great form that year and was our top scorer as we strolled through another Connacht campaign. I hit a goal and three points in both games as we beat Tourlestrane and then hammered Leitrim champions St Mary's-Kiltoghert in the semi-finals. It was all too easy for us and it was difficult to tell whether we still had the stomach for a real battle.

The other semi-final saw Castlebar Mitchels pull of a surprise win over Corofin. We knew we would be in for a tough day at the Hyde, but we were also confident that we were a better side than Castlebar. We just never predicted referee Marty Duffy sending three of us off.

WE HAD STARTED that game really well too, playing some brilliant football in the first-half before the wheels came off at the very end of normal time in the second. We must have missed two goals and five points in the opening half.

Duffy's decision to overrule his linesman and award Castlebar a lineball would lead to Ian Kilbride receiving a red card for a clumsy tackle in front our posts. Castlebar tied the game up and their fitness would tell in extra-time. But not before Darragh Donnelly and Richie Blaine were also given their marching orders.

We were sickened at the end of it and I was falsely accused of striking the linesman whose decision had been overturned by Duffy. A very bad end to a bad day.

As I've already said, the initial 48-week ban I received for the incident at full-time that day probably would have forced me into retirement. Thankfully, my suspension was halved on appeal because it would have broken my heart to end my career in such a negative way.

I was also lucky at that stage to be still playing under Benny O'Brien, Liam McHale and Phil O'Reilly, because they were quick to realise that some of us older lads were running out of road. They were really understanding and designed training schedules that allowed us to play on for another year.

THE ENFORCED REST was welcome in early 2014 and I felt refreshed when I did get back playing in the championship. To be honest, in the county final against St Faithleach's that year I felt as fit as I ever did and ended up with a goal and eight points. Senan was still going strong of course and he ended up with two goals and a point. It was all too easy again though and we completed our 'Drive for Five' without ever really being tested. I had now won a total of 10 county titles, including one Longford title with Ballymahon.

Connacht would once again prove to be a step too far for us, however, and we were beaten by three points by Mayo champions Ballintubber in the semi-final. That year heralded the beginning of Corofin's dominance in the competition and they hammered Leitrim side Aughawillan in their semi-final, scoring seven goals and 20 points in the process. Ballintubber would also prove no match for them in the final as the Galway champions won the first of their five titles in six years.

Benny, Liam and Phil must have seen what was coming down the tracks because they stepped down after our defeat to Ballintubber. The club had entered a major period of transition and the next man in the hot seat would need to be prepared to take on a long-term rebuilding project. It was a formidable task.

THERE WAS SOME surprise then when Donegal's Paddy Carr was ratified as our new manager in late 2014. Paddy had won an All-Ireland club title with Kilmacud Crokes in 2009 and had also managed Louth. He had also been in the running for the Donegal job after Jim McGuinness stepped down. He had the pedigree, but he was based up near Dublin at the time and I think that really hampered him.

In truth, it was a disappointing year for all of us.

The morale around the place was at an all-time low, something which had seemed impossible only a year before. There just wasn't the same motivation or commitment and that was partly down to how things were being run.

Paddy was a gentleman, a really lovely fella, but the players had become used to certain standards and expected the management team to live up to them. We could nearly train ourselves by that stage, but we were used to top-class sessions and clear communication from the top down, and Paddy and his team didn't offer us that, I felt.

To put it bluntly, it had become a bit farcical at times, especially when it came to the training sessions. I just felt that there was no thought put into what we were doing, and it seemed like there was no real plan in place. There was no cohesion that year at all.

We would be set up and ready to do a drill and then it would just stop abruptly, and we'd move on to something else. The sessions had a stop-start feel to them and players began to get frustrated. I said the morale was low, but the atmosphere around the club was the worst I had ever experienced too. I think some of the players were beginning to get completely fed up and it was openly acknowledged that the whole set-up had become a bit of a shambles.

Something had to give in a dressing-room like that. There were a few of us coming towards the end of our careers and running out of time too.

It wasn't worth sticking around.

A group of players put together a dossier detailing their grievances over training, as well as the overall management of the team. I didn't know anything about it, and I asked Karol Mannion and some of the other senior players about it at the time and they were also in the dark.

This group had taken it upon themselves to put pen to paper and list our most common complaints each week.

That's when the whole situation really went downhill.

I had no problem with what they did – they were only trying to improve a bad situation. But it was the way they went about it which rankled some of the senior players and put us in direct confrontation with management.

I REMEMBER GETTING ready in the dressing-room before training one evening and Paddy arrived in, very unhappy. Could you blame him? He and the chairman Michael McDonnell started reading this dossier out to all of us, steam coming out of Paddy's ears.

That's when the shit really hit the fan.

It created two groups in the dressing-room – the lads who had put the list together and the other lads who had kept quiet and got on with it. I was in the latter group because no matter how bad I thought a session was – and I thought a few of them were poor – I always gave one hundred percent.

Others felt the same, but clearly the standards had dropped and a few of us had become disillusioned. I could understand both sides, of course I could, but the fallout afterwards was of no benefit to us.

Paddy was unfortunate with injuries that year too, but I suppose that was bound to happen with the age profile of the team. We reached the semi-finals of the Roscommon championship where we were beaten by Clann na nGael of all teams. I remember leaving the field that day, thinking back to my first county title in 1997 and all the success we had enjoyed since then. I didn't want it to end like this.

Clann went on to win their 20th title and shortly afterwards Michael O'Donnell announced that Paddy was no longer available to remain in charge. It felt like my time had finally come to an end too and I was stressing over what I would do next.

As a player for over 20 years, I had developed a routine based around midweek training and preparing for matches at the weekend. It is not easy to transition into something else and I was worried I'd go out of my mind without football to look forward to each week.

It's not all about the football either.

The thing I still miss most about it is the craic of it all. Your teammates and the people you meet along the way make Gaelic football what it is. You see it in those player profiles in match programmes all the time.

Players are asked, 'What's the best thing about the GAA?'

It doesn't matter whether you're Stephen Cluxton or a lad making up the numbers in Junior B, the answer is usually something along the lines of… 'The friends you make'.

Some people might read it and think it's a forced answer or some sort of cliché but trust me, it's not.

THE BANTER WAS always mighty in the St Brigid's dressing- room and it's something that I think I'll always miss. There was nothing too clever about it, just the usual bullshit that lads go on with. Slagging after mad nights out and stuff like that. Though as time went on, I was less likely to be at the centre of it all.

I forget a lot of the matches I've played in and even some of the big scores, but I'll never forget the scene each night as we prepared to tog out for training.

The session would usually start at eight o'clock on the button, but I'd arrive in early to have the craic with Pat Regan, who remains a great friend of mine to this day. Senan was usually next in the door at twenty-five past seven.

You'd nearly be able to set your watch to when each of the lads would show up. Some of them would come fully togged, while others would be still in their work clothes.

I'd have Garvan sitting on my left.

And the first thing he usually did was to look for Mango to have a go at him over something. Those two had a strange relationship, they would tear ribbons out of each other over different things, but they'd always have each other's backs too.

Garvan would never admit it, but he missed Karol when he wasn't around. How do I know this? Because he put so much time and energy into slagging him!

One of Garvan's favourite routines was to wait for the county lads to return to the club after Roscommon had been knocked out of the championship. Some of us wouldn't know what to say to them after a bad defeat, but good old Garv was there to break the ice the minute they walked in the door. The likes of Mango and the Kilbrides would hardly be sitting down and he'd start.

'Well, thank Christ that county shite is over for another year!'

Karol would sit there trying to ignore him, while Ian and Senan might burst out laughing and have a go back at him. It was all just part of the game.

It's definitely the craic with teammates that I miss most, and not even management can replicate that. Kevin McStay's words in Croke Park always come back to me.

'Ye will be at each other's funerals.'

You develop a strong bond with each other and it's something that will never be fully broken.

AS FOR PLAYING the game itself, I've often compared it to being on some wonderful drug. The adrenaline you feel on your way out the door to matches becomes just as addictive anyway.

For a long time, I worried about how I would spend my evenings and weekends after it was all over. Would I be one of those guys walking around Athlone Town Centre or Ganly's Hardware Store on a Saturday morning?

That didn't sound too appealing to me.

Stepping away from it can leave a very empty feeling and I know that it has led some retired sportspeople to question their identity or even their self-worth afterwards. Spending the weekend walking around a DIY store just doesn't compare to running out in front of thousands of people at Kiltoom, the Hyde or even Croke Park.

There's just nothing like being in the dressing-room an hour before a big match either, togging out in silence as you prepare for battle. There might even be a few butterflies. But then I look around the dressing-room at my teammates.

Shane Curran.

John Whyte... Clifford McDonald.

'Dixie' O'Brien.

Peter Domican... Garvan and Darren... Karol Mannion.

David 'Jimmy Nail' O'Connor.

The Lennons.

Niall Grehan... Tom Óg O'Brien... Mixer Ryan.

Fergal O'Donnell... Nigel Dineen... Francie Grehan... Johnny Dunning.

Conor Connelly.

The Kilbrides. The Lohans.

And the next new face... and the next...

It didn't matter where I was, I always seemed to be surrounded by top men.

I lived for that moment when it came time to stream out onto the pitch one after the other.

The roar of the supporters hits you and the hair stands up on the back of your neck.

Adrenaline pumping through your veins as you head out to your position.

You welcome your man with a shoulder.

The ball is thrown up.

Brief silence.

One of our lads grabs it.

The… ROAR!

I can still feel it now.

PART SIX

Sunset and Sideline

« CHAPTER 21 »

WHEN IT CAME down to it, I just couldn't bring myself to walk away from St Brigid's, especially after the disappointment of the year before. There were a few names in the running to take over from Paddy Carr at the end of 2015, but I really fancied a crack at it.

Caroline thought I was stone mad!

At this stage, I had very little coaching experience, but I decided I'd call the chairman Mike McDonnell anyway and let him know how badly I wanted the job. I had been working with the Roscommon under-21s in 2015 but my CV was nowhere near as impressive as the likes of McStay or Paddy Carr.

Mike assumed that I'd still be playing the following year and, for a brief moment, had no idea what I was talking about on the phone.

In fairness to him, as soon as the penny dropped, he agreed to hear me out and I made my case. I don't know whether it was my passionate plea or that I knew the club inside out and was living close by, but Mike agreed to put my name forward and that's something I'll always be grateful for.

The fact that it was St Brigid's meant it was an opportunity I couldn't resist. I knew that it was a huge first job for a novice manager. We're not talking about some Mickey Mouse outfit after all.

But I really believed I could be the man to take us back to the top.

I was clever about it too and surrounded myself with great football men right from the start. I brought in a good right-hand man in Eddie Lohan, and an experienced coach in Ger Dowd. The two lads did some great work in my time there and helped make that transition from player to manager much easier.

TAKING ON THE responsibility of managing a big club like St Brigid's was difficult enough, but I had to remember that I had a young family to look after also. I'd be away from the house quite a bit between training and matches and the many other commitments that come with one of the biggest jobs in Roscommon football.

My days suddenly became much longer too. I'd set off for work with An Post at half past six each morning, work my shift, and then have to be in Kiltoom for seven o'clock two evenings a week to prepare training sessions. I seriously underestimated the amount of time I'd spend on the phone throughout the week too. But I knew that to be successful I'd have to put the hours in.

It's also important that players see you taking it seriously. When they see you arriving early for training and taking the time to set up proper sessions then there's a trickle-down effect and it creates a proper culture at the club.

Actions always speak louder than words.

While I was putting in the hours developing the youth at St Brigid's I was missing my own boys as they were growing up. I was incredibly lucky that I had a great wife in Caroline, who understood what football meant to me and that it was something I loved doing. A man could be at a lot worse I suppose.

AS A FORMER player, I believed I had an advantage over anyone coming from outside the club. I knew all about the issues from the year before and I could also see that the current Brigid's' team was coming to the end of the line.

On the other hand, I knew there was great potential in the younger players and another year or two left for the more senior lads. There were also a couple of lads breaking through at that time who would push us on a bit. We were certainly good enough. It was just a matter of getting the lads on board and putting together a good management team to give us the structure and cohesion that was lacking the year before.

There were big decisions to make, and that's why it's important when you're the manager that a wall goes up between you and your former teammates. I couldn't show favouritism to my brothers Garvan and Darren, or to the likes of Mango, the Kilbrides, Peter Domican or any of the other lads I had soldiered with before.

The lads knew I wouldn't operate like that anyway and that I had to keep my distance in order to remain fair.

In fairness to the lads, they respected me and appreciated that it wasn't an easy job. It made the transition from being 'one of the lads' to managing the team that bit easier for me. The players bought into it from the start and it wasn't long before we were back enjoying ourselves once again.

THERE WERE A few changes that year with lads stepping away. Karol Mannion was also coming to the end of an illustrious career and there were a couple more in that bracket as well.

The time was right to introduce some fresh blood into the mix and the players that came in went on to become pillars of the successful Brigid's teams in 2016 and '17 and 2020. Fellas like Eddie Nolan and Brian Stack have also gone on to represent Roscommon in recent years and that gave us great satisfaction.

I always tried to be fair during my three years in charge at the club and I'd like to believe the players appreciated that. It was a stressful job though and there were times when I felt like walking away. Some of the lads coming up had different attitudes to training than I would have had.

Football was secondary to them and that's something I struggled to get my head around. Maybe I was the one with the problem!

I brought in a local personal trainer Anthony Jinks for strength and conditioning and he was a revelation from the beginning. Jinksy has since been part of any management team I've been involved with because he's top-class. I'd like to think I know a lot about Gaelic football, but I wouldn't have had a clue about the strength and conditioning side of the game. I've done a couple of courses in the meantime and I have gained a better understanding of it, but someone like Jinksy is still invaluable.

Eddie Lohan and Ger Dowd were great support also. The pieces were in place for us to go and have a good year.

TAKING CHARGE OF your first training session has a different feel to running out onto the pitch as a player. I was probably more nervous the night I made my way down to the club that first evening than I had been running out at Croke Park!

As is customary for any new manager, I was expected to have a chat with the lads and 'introduce' myself and my backroom team. That was a weird feeling.

Apart from the fact that the lads already knew me and most of the management team, I always felt that most of those 'new manager' chats were pure bullshit. It's usually just a fella talking for the sake of it, and I think most players see through that.

I always look to keep things nice and simple, so that lads can go out and enjoy playing football. Now don't get me wrong, I expect lads to train hard and if we're doing a skills session, for example, I want lads to be fully focused on it. Even if it's not going right for them, I expect them to keep at it until they improve. Improvement always takes time and repetitive practice.

It's also important to have structure to training sessions and any of the conditioning work I do is based on the data we collect during games. I don't believe in running for the sake of it and most of our drills were based around moving at pace with the ball. That way players are getting miles in their legs, while also getting more comfortable in possession.

Good defending is also a priority for me and there's nothing worse than players giving away soft frees for lazy tackling or being caught out of position.

It drives me to distraction.

We also got through loads of shooting drills. They weren't just aimed at the forwards either, the whole team can benefit from being comfortable in front of the posts. The game has evolved so much in recent years that it's nearly like a seven-a-side now. The forwards must be comfortable defensively, and the backs should be expected to contribute when further forward.

Those first few sessions confirmed what I believed; that we had a team capable of competing in Roscommon and even winning a county title. We had lads coming up from minor who could also make a difference. Conor Murray was six foot three and a good addition to the team. I enjoyed putting in the work with young lads like Conor as they made their transition to senior football.

While there were impressive youngsters coming up through the ranks, some of the more senior players were coming near the end. There would have to be a few adjustments.

Karol Mannion, for example, was one of the finest midfielders our club had ever produced but I took him aside and offered an honest assessment of where I thought he was at. We had good lads coming through, like Eddie Nolan, who went on to play senior county, and Mark Daly. Also Conor Murray, aswell as Garvan and Ian Kilbride. We had a lot of options in the middle, and I wanted to strengthen our forward line further – Mango had played up front for the club and county before. I knew he could excel there too.

I was bracing myself for his reaction but thankfully he seemed to understand.

That was a tough part of the job, but you owe it to yourself and the players to make the hard decisions.

I had no worries about Mango, I knew he would adapt. He still had a lot to offer the team, but we had to utilise him in the right way to get the best out of him.

I changed it that year and pushed him up into the full-forward line where I thought he was excellent for us alongside Senan. We had given him a free role in this area with a focus on getting on as much ball as possible. Just stay inside and give teams the headache of having to mark you, we told him. He seemed to enjoy it.

Eddie Nolan was another player enjoying his football in 2016. It was hard to believe it was only his first year. Mark Daly was excellent too. These were lads that had just come into the team but Eddie Lohan and myself had put a lot of work in with them to prepare them for the demands of senior football.

They repaid us with interest that year too. They were athletic, strong and above all hungry. They made a huge difference to the whole panel.

I HAD A good first year in management with St Brigid's. Our performances that year confirmed my belief that we had not become a bad team overnight and that 2015 was just a poor year for us.

You couldn't have written a better script either.

We reached the county final where we met Pádraig Pearses, who had my former teammate Shane 'Cake' Curran, over them. To add to the excitement, Dr Hyde Park was out of action that year so the final would be played at our home pitch in Kiltoom.

I WOULD CONSIDER Cake a great buddy of mine and we'd still be in close contact to this day, but there was a strict 'radio silence' in the build-up to that final.

To add to the pressure, the game was broadcast live on TG4 and I remember being a bit nervous in the weeks leading up to it.

It had little to do with being on television either, I just didn't think we really performed well in Kiltoom. The pitch was a bit on the small side, and I felt the Hyde would have suited our expansive style of football better. Forget home advantage, the venue would play right into Pearses' hands as they got man, woman and child behind the ball. I was so worried about it that I approached the Chairman Michael McDonnell and told him we needed to widen the pitch to give ourselves more space. It was only extended by about a metre on each side, but it was enough to give our lads a slight psychological boost.

The week of the final though we slightly exaggerated the change in dimensions and that seemed to get Pearses' backs up – or at least Cake's anyway! He had been down to see the pitch a couple of weeks before the final, something that didn't go down too well in the club.

I lost count of the number of people asking who let the lunatic in and what he was doing there. The mind games had really started at that stage.

We arrived down to training one Tuesday evening and one of the lads from the club came running over. He looked like he had seen a ghost.

'Frankie, there's red and white markings around the pitch…!'

Sure enough, someone had marked the railings which ran around the outside of the pitch in the Pearses' colours. This led to lots of speculation in the run-up to the final as to what they could have been, but it didn't really bother me.

I assumed it was to do with the Pearses' kick-out strategy or else it was just Cake trying to get into our heads.

A couple of years later he told me that they were for the defensive and shooting set-up, for marking where his players should push out to. Thankfully, our players usually remembered these things without any amateur artwork.

It did annoy me that he had been allowed into our pitch in the first place. He was a feckin' blow-in from Castlerea, who was now managing our near neighbours in a county final against us, and yet here he was daubing graffiti all over our turf!

It wasn't just Kiltoom that had featured some of 'Banksy' Curran's work either. The Roscommon Gaels manager, Liam McNeill had complained about it earlier in the year too and so had a few others.

But that's just Cake, he'd try anything to get that little edge. We just hoped he wasn't bringing the Vaseline or a bag of his own blood.

Shane Curran is like Marmite to people – you either love him or you hate him. I love him, because, while he might be a bit mad, at least he's his own man.

Having said that, there are probably plenty of people who don't have much time for me either, but you try not to lose too much sleep over it. One thing is for sure, whenever we played together you would have struggled to find two other men who would give more for the cause, whether it was for Brigid's or Roscommon.

Cake was also one of the outstanding goalkeepers of his generation and that's something that gets overlooked. I still regard him as one of the best in the business, and as the very best I've played with or against.

Keep in mind too that I've togged out with the likes of the Dublin legend, Stephen Cluxton. Cake was just outrageous in his heyday; he was just so talented. There's no doubt in my mind that in terms of reflexes and kickouts he was the very best in the country on his day.

He was a real winner... well, except in that county final in 2016.

IT'S FUNNY WHAT pops into your head on the day of a big match.

I knew that the television camera was going to be near enough to ground level between the two dugouts. I also knew that Cake would be roaring and shouting, and pacing up and down the line like some sort of caged animal.

I felt it would be better for our players and supporters if I kept my cool and avoided too much national television exposure. Plus, the game was going to be beamed into houses across the country and I just didn't want to come across as some sort of eejit.

Just before the game, I pulled Eddie Lohan aside.

'You're wearing the manager's bib and I'll take your one,' I told him.

'Ah Frankie, sure it's your first county final...' He was taken aback but I just wanted to be able to watch the game without the distraction of Cake roaring and shouting.

I made my way around to the far side of the pitch with Patsy O'Connor and we watched the first-half from there. Even with the extra wide pitch and the big crowd in Kiltoom that day, I could still hear that lunatic Cake barking instructions at his players.

Poor Eddie even complained of a headache at half-time.

As for the game itself, we played great football and we should have put it to bed much earlier on. Mango put a penalty over the bar and we probably invited some needless pressure on ourselves, but Darragh Donnelly and Ian Kilbride scored two late goals and we ran out comfortable winners in the end.

While I was proud of the lads and proud of myself for winning my first title as a manager, there was an incident towards the end which probably took a bit of the gloss off it.

Garvan got caught up in a scrap with a couple of the Daly brothers so, as his big brother, I decided to sub myself on to back him up. It wasn't long before I was wrestling on the ground with one of them while Garvan and Niall Daly started going at it too. A real brotherly Royal Rumble.

Poor Garvan had probably earned the Man of the Match award up to that point but Niall and himself were both sent off. It was a nothing offence really and I can't help but feel at least partly responsible for him being denied the limelight.

Then again, he did say he didn't really like the limelight all those years ago when he turned down the captaincy ahead of our All-Ireland semi-final against Nemo Rangers. Serves him right I suppose!

I ENJOYED PROVING a few people wrong in 2016.

It was a nice feeling to see things we had worked on in training coming together on the pitch. Some people mightn't realise the amount of effort that goes into the sessions each week or the tactical analysis needed to prepare a senior team to compete in a county championship, never mind win one.

The whole Dolan clan was at the game that day too and it was a wonderful feeling to be able to share the moment with them. It was a proud day for all of us and it was nice to be able to enjoy the celebrations fully too.

I didn't really expect to win a Connacht club title in my first year as manager, but our confidence grew after the hiding we gave Leitrim side Aughawillan in the semi-final. Things really clicked that day in Carrick-on-Shannon and there was no reason why we couldn't upset the mighty Corofin in the final.

It would turn out to be very wishful thinking on our part though, and we were annihilated by the Galway champions at Pairc Seán Mac Diarmada. There was no real shame in losing that match because that Corofin side was probably the best club football has ever seen. They would have beaten most county sides at that stage too.

I'M USUALLY CONFIDENT going into matches, but I got a bad feeling just before throw in that day. Our dressing-room is normally buzzing for big games with lads having the craic and the usual slagging as they get togged out or receive last minute physio treatment. But there was a different vibe to it in Carrick and the pre-match preparation proved as much.

'This is not good… not good at all,' I muttered to Eddie Lohan and Ger Dowd, as we watched what was probably our worst warm-up of the year. The boys were nervous, you could see it in them.

We got them back into the dressing-room and I tried my best to spark some life or bite into them. 'Lads, we really need to buck up here. This isn't us. We're the Roscommon champions for f**k sake… liven it up!'

My appeal probably came a bit too late. The tension had set in and it affected us mentally and physically.

In fairness to Corofin, they were ruthless too and it probably wouldn't have made a huge difference in terms of the result had we gone in as our usual confident selves. As it stood, they beat us back down the N60 and any notions we had of regaining the Connacht title had disappeared into thin air.

ONE OF MY strangest memories of taking training sessions in Kiltoom was when the club hosted the Sheep Shearing Championships in 2017 and the new pitch was taken over by sheep gates and other obstacles. The entire senior team was forced to train within the '45' one night.

There was an underage team training that night too and they had about 20 footballs thrown to the side while the managers made them run around the sheep gates and hurdles. They didn't see a football for a good hour, which was alien to me.

It seems obvious, but to become a good footballer you need to be working with the ball. Ask any of the great modern footballers, the likes of Diarmuid Connolly or 'Gooch' Cooper and they'll tell you they were rarely without a football.

My own mother will tell you that I was constantly carrying or kicking a football as soon as I could walk. My sister still slags me over taking the ball to bed with me!

The gable end of our home house is only now recovering from all my hours of practice. Kids these days don't do enough of that kind of practice, so training should be all about the football.

Take it from someone who knows, it's difficult, if not impossible to teach an adult the basic skills such as kicking and hand passing off both sides. Those foundations have to be laid in childhood.

Even when I was over the Rosemount team in 2020, I found that we had to strip training back to basic underage drills because there were lads who hadn't been trained to use their weaker foot. It wasn't a minority of them either; I would say about ninety percent of them were ineffective on their weak side.

To me, that's just unacceptable and it must be something to do with the club structure and the emphasis on winning. What are these teams doing in training at underage level? Were they like those Brigid's under-8s and under-10s running around sheep gates without a football?

I watch my two boys Ryen and Jack playing with Roscommon Gaels and it's amazing how quickly they learn to become comfortable on their weaker foot.

But it's important to keep at them because all players tend to take shortcuts. You'd nearly be pulling your hair out sometimes but that's part of coaching, and some of the adult teams can be even more frustrating!

« CHAPTER 22 »

THE LIFE OF a manager is far more stressful than that of a player with all the different responsibilities you have. I wasn't long in the job at St Brigid's before I gained an appreciation of how much work is involved in running a senior team.

As well as the usual stuff like putting together training sessions, fitness plans and tactical briefings, there were other day-to-day headaches that I hadn't even thought about as a player. It was stressful at times just trying to make sure players could make it to training sessions, especially those who were working or studying away from home. The logistics involved for a rural club in a county like Roscommon mean that you're starting out at a disadvantage before a ball is even kicked.

There were lads arriving straight from college and work in Dublin sometimes, who hadn't even managed to get a bit of food into them before training. It got to the stage where I was ordering meals for them from a filling station on the Athlone Road so they would have something to eat in the car on the way home. It wasn't the healthiest food in the world, but it had to be better than nothing.

We were left with little choice at times. There were weeks when we had to practically beg lads to make the journey down so that we'd have the numbers for training.

Each week was the same.

I'd text lads and ask them what they wanted… then I'd ring Supermacs with the order. Some of the younger lads would nearly be too shy to tell you but you couldn't have them driving home late at night on an empty stomach, especially after a tough session.

The meals would be ready for them when they finished at half nine and they'd eat them on the way back to Dublin.

It wasn't just weekly meals I was supplying either.

I WAS SITTING in the dressing-room one evening going over that night's session when a few of the lads landed in to get togged. I couldn't get over the state of some of the gear on show. Some of them were playing in boots that were coming apart at the seams, just bits of tape holding them together.

'Ah lads!' was all I could say.

It was a long time since I'd seen anything like it.

After training had finished, I took three of them aside and quietly asked them for their boot sizes. If anyone could understand being short a few quid for football training, it was me. As a young fella I had always received great support from the older players and now it was my turn to pay it forward.

That weekend I went into George Bannon in Roscommon town and bought three brand new pairs of boots. The following Tuesday I handed them to the boys discreetly.

They were a little embarrassed, but they had no reason to be. Studying and working while trying to make training sessions and maintain the St Brigid's' standards was not easy and I was happy to be able to help in any way I could.

The club is a family after all.

It works both ways too, and to me that's the kind of thing that gets these young players on your side. They remember that and they'll work extra hard for you. They know I can be trusted and when things get tough in a big game, I know they'll repay that trust. Creating that kind of atmosphere brings the team closer together. You need that camaraderie in a dressing-room.

The times have changed since I first entered a senior dressing-room. Young lads these days have so much going on that football isn't the be-all and end-all anymore. There are other distractions out there and most lads are now working away from Roscommon, so the closeness we had as players doesn't come as naturally as it used to.

The youth of today also have more power than we ever did. There's no such thing as blind faith in authority these days and they know full well what they're entitled to. But at the end of the day there can only be one boss, both on the pitch and in the workplace. They must learn quickly that to get respect, they must give it too.

Overall, Gaelic players have more clout these days compared to what I had as a youngster. Managers 'losing the dressing-room' is nothing new but it can be harder to keep this current generation in line.

I MUST ADMIT that I experienced some of that in my last year with St Brigid's. I just had a sneaking suspicion that one or two weren't doing what I wanted them to. Just little things here and there, like straying from their positions or not doing enough of the dirty work. To me, that's absolute bullshit.

You might think it's hypocritical for me to give out about players being on a different wavelength to their manager, but I always played for the jersey no matter how much I disliked or disagreed with some of mine.

Yes, there were plenty of arguments and sometimes it was easier to walk away but at training or out on the pitch I gave it my all and did whatever was asked of me. The way I see it, if you've got a problem with a manager then let them know, otherwise shut up and give one hundred percent for the team.

It's at the stage now though where you can't say anything remotely critical to some lads, but I think that's just society in general. People are too easily offended these days.

You even have to be careful when commenting on social media just in case it's taken up wrong. I think we've gone too soft and too politically correct, if I'm honest, and young fellas know they can get away with more.

Some of them have lost that respect for authority and while a certain amount of that is healthy, it can have a negative effect overall.

On the pitch, I used some reverse psychology to get some of the more stubborn ones to do what I asked. I'd nearly be telling them to do the exact opposite of what I wanted and in some cases it worked. It would really make you think about what goes through their heads.

Some of it could be down to them getting everything done for them at home too. You had to be a man in our dressing-room back in 1997 but in 2017 things were a bit different. Some of these young fellas are spoilt in comparison.

I remember walking into Kiltoom one evening and one of the younger lads was sitting in the kitchen at half seven eating a full meal.

Mammy had brought the dinner down for him and here he was, tucking in 30 minutes before training!

'What are you at?' I asked.

'Just eating the dinner,' he replied, cool as you like.

'I see that. Is she coming back with the trifle?'

He let out a little laugh and carried on.

There was no laughing half an hour later when I ran the backside off him. That's just the way it is with some of the younger lads though. You wouldn't have had that problem with Karol Mannion or Senan Kilbride or the Lennons. It was only a small minority of the young fellas but sometimes I could only scratch my head and wonder where we had all gone wrong.

WHILE THERE WERE plenty of headaches, I really enjoyed the coaching side of managing St Brigid's. It was great to be still involved on the pitch and passing on any knowledge I had.

As manager, there's a lot of non-football stuff that drives me insane. Like sending out texts for training, trying to get them to eat their dinners and dressing them properly – you'd swear I was their mammy sometimes!

There were times when those management headaches got the better of me and I wanted to pack it in. I just felt there were times when lads were slacking off. Maybe they just weren't as intense or obsessed about it as I was or just showed it a different way.

I had enough in 2018 with text messages coming the evening of a training session, maybe around 7.30pm, and we training at 8pm. I said to Patsy and the caretaker at the time Val Lynch that I was done, I was resigning. I could not deal with it any longer and I had my bag packed up, and was gone out the door, when Val grabbed me and tried talking with me. He told me I could not step away.

I valued Val's opinion, and I turned around, and put the gear back on and took the session. But I remained angry with some players, and their lack of commitment to the team. Looking back now with a clear head, however, I would have had no regrets had I kept walking.

I stormed out of the dressing-room on a couple of occasions. I even threatened to walk away completely once, until one of the club officials caught hold of me and told me to calm down.

But the coaching was all about football and helping them to improve as players. That was the part I loved. Even now, I'm constantly trying to evolve as a coach and thinking about different ways of playing the game and different training methods. I still love the game now as much as I ever did.

I also didn't want to leave the game I loved to some of the spoofers I had seen down through the years. Some of the training that coaches are at even now is absolute bullshit to me. There are also managers out there who just run the shite out of teams but have no real idea of how to train them.

It's not long before players see through that and lose their enjoyment of it.

There must be a structure and goals laid out throughout the year. You should always be working towards something, whether it's fitness or skills related. I always try to encourage players to be comfortable on both sides of their bodies... right foot, left foot... right hand, left hand. They should be helped to learn positional sense and how to perfect their individual roles.

Most importantly though, they should be confident in expressing themselves. Some managers roar at players when they try something and it doesn't come off. There's no sense to that because unless you take some risks you will never develop.

My coaching is based on how I learned the game.

Some of my managers tore their hair out over it, but if I didn't try outrageous passes or shots then I never would have had the confidence to take important scores in big games. The opposition would have turned over possession while I delayed, or some other eejit would have kicked it 20 yards wide!

It's a simple game and I don't want my teams to overcomplicate it or shy away from a challenge. I want them to have a go and if it comes off that's great. If it doesn't, then I'll be the last man getting on their backs about it.

EVERYTHING SEEMED TO come full circle at the end of my time in the St Brigid's' hot seat. My club football career had started with a county final win over our fierce rivals Clann na nGael in 1997 when I was just 19. My time as manager came to an end in 2018 when we were on the wrong side of the result in a county final against Clann.

I felt we had squeezed every last bit of effort out of the lads over the three seasons I had been in charge. We made it back to the top of the Roscommon football tree in 2016 after Clann had won their 20th title in '15. We then managed to close the gap on Clann even further with our 16th title in 2017. That was important for the club and our supporters.

We were going well in the 2018 showdown and it even looked like another three in-a-row was on before one of the club stalwarts Gearoid Cunniffe was sent off. We just lost our shape after that and the game slipped away from us, which was very disappointing.

There were other near misses and 'what might have been' moments during my tenure too. We took the great Corofin team to extra-time in 2017 and if we had been a bit more clinical you never know what might have happened.

Beating Corofin in Connacht would certainly have given us the belief to go on and have a crack at the All-Ireland series too. Those are the fine margins at play, and sadly for us, we just didn't get the rub of the green. Though the effort the players put in that day made me very proud of them.

I COULD NEVER fault the lads' efforts throughout my stint as manager. Sure, there might have been some frustration at times when it came to getting lads down for training but once they were there, most of them gave it their all.

I tried to drum it into the younger players that if they wanted to win anything or be successful in life, then they had to put the work in and be committed.

Showing up to training late and jogging around half-arsed wasn't going to cut it with me.

That's the way I operate, and I expect my players to buy into that.

St Brigid's lost a lot of great leaders in the last few years and so those young players have had to step up. There were a couple of years when there were players at the club who just didn't have it in them to drive younger players on and so the senior team went into transition.

This was nothing new and the club has gone through lean periods before; the years between 1997 and '05 were even worse. You'll always have two or three years when you don't win anything but it's important to stick together so that you can build a team.

It was always going to be difficult for the likes of Brian and Ronan Stack and Peter Domican to take on leadership roles, but their county title win in 2020 proved they're more than capable.

In recent years, Corofin set the benchmark for what it takes to be successful at club level. From my experience, you earn your own luck by taking it seriously and having lads who are fully committed to the cause.

It's give and take too.

Occasionally, it's fine if a fella wants to head out for a couple of pints or for a bit of dinner. Players need a break from training and football so they can recharge.

You need that balance because it prevents lads from suffering burn-out and means they look forward to the sessions rather than seeing them as a burden. It also helps to keep the wives and partners onside too!

Striking that balance is something I have introduced at other clubs I've worked with. Having that time off is important for mental health. Having down time and hobbies away from football is not only healthy, but it can also benefit performance.

I'VE ALWAYS HAD fishing and shooting to take my mind off work and football. Both pastimes give me the opportunity to switch off the phone and get some head space. I'm out in the fresh air to escape from the world for a while.

The only conversation I'll have is with the dog, and he doesn't say that much.

Golf is something else I really enjoy but things change when you have kids and when Ryen came along the clubs were put away. I still get the odd weekend away each year but with two young lads playing sport and my own football commitments, it's harder to find the time.

There was a time when I was a member in Roscommon as well as Athlone, and was playing off a handicap of about 12, so I wasn't too bad I suppose. I was only really getting into the swing of it when I stopped playing regularly.

I used to meet up with one of my colleagues in An Post Mickey Craven who has since sadly passed away. We would go out and play nine or 12 holes after we finished our shifts in Roscommon. It was something I really enjoyed, and Mickey was great company.

We left the phones in the car and off we went.

The only thing to annoy us on those days was the golf ball.

IN MY SECOND year at St Brigid's, the opportunity came up for Senan

Kilbride to go and play football in the United States. These offers are always there for players but often they're turned down due to club or county commitments.

This time I encouraged Senan to go.

He was surprised but I knew it was something he wanted to do the previous few years and I just felt that it was something he deserved to experience. I also knew I could trust him.

Senan could be counted on to go and enjoy himself in America but come back in good shape. Not every lad could be trusted to do the same. Some would be back in time for the championship, but they wouldn't be fit to carry the water bottles.

Not Senan. He was in constant contact with me throughout his stay, asking me what kind of training the team was doing and what I wanted him to be doing.

'Just go and enjoy yourself... and do a bit each day,' I told him, and that's all I needed to say. He had already sacrificed so much for Brigid's, a few months away was the least he deserved.

That's the difference between a Senan Kilbride and Karol Mannion and your average player. The spoofers and the lads who put in the minimal amount of effort are starting to get found out though, even at club level. It has gone so professional in some places that there just aren't any hiding places anymore.

Maybe I'm biased towards him, but Senan was one-of-a-kind. I don't think St Brigid's had a wealth of natural forwards during my time there, but I felt that myself and Senan were two I'd put in that bracket. I'm not too sure the club will see a partnership like that again either, not in terms of longevity anyway.

I hope I'm wrong of course, but that level of natural talent, combined with total commitment to Gaelic football, only comes along so often.

I'M STILL PROUD when I look back on my time as St Brigid's manager. I took the job for the right reasons. Getting the club back to the top was what drove me in those three years. It was a demanding job and you do need to be slightly obsessed with the game if you want to be successful.

From the moment I woke up in the morning, I was thinking about players, team selection, training and a million and one other things all the way through until my head hit the pillow again that night.

There was no financial incentive driving this obsessive behaviour either. Sure,

I received some expenses and the odd family holiday, but the compensation was nowhere near what some other managers were getting from clubs.

For me, the greatest reward was seeing your team be successful due to the work you had done behind the scenes. I took the job to win things, not to make money or to get free holidays.

In fact, there were probably times when it cost me money to manage St Brigid's, but it was a small price to pay for the honour.

Taking charge of the club I loved and helping them to win back-to-back county titles in 2016 and '17 will always be right up there with any of my proudest moments in sport.

In every club in Ireland there is always one clubman who is a legend in that club, and in St Brigid's that man for me is PJ Martin. PJ has taken up every role in the club since the 80s. From club chairman, to the clubman who 'finds' and 'borrows' footballs, or simply 'forgets' to return footballs to the opposing team.

PJ has his very own press in the clubhouse where he keeps his stash, though nobody has ever seen inside it. When I was manager, occasionally I would ask him for a few balls and I would purposely follow him, to get a look into his 'safe'.

But even when I was in the room with him, I couldn't see everything.

Once, when we were playing in a game broadcast live from Castlebar, the television cameras picked up on the fact that we had a football in our possession which, clear as day, had 'Crossmaglen' written across it. That led to some craic – and also an enquiry from my good friend Oisin McConville, wondering if we would be sending their ball back to Cross.

PJ? His reply was, 'Sure, didn't they get enough off us over the years!'

PJ is still hard at work in the club to this day and central, with Sean Kilbride, behind the new development that will be commencing very soon. The man loves his club. Plus, he has always supported me personally, and I will always be grateful to PJ for that, and his brilliant friendship.

« CHAPTER 23 »

I STEPPED DOWN as St Brigid's manager shortly after our county final defeat in 2018. I just felt I had taken the team as far as I could and that it was time to move on. The three years of managerial duties had been intense too and I was looking forward to a break from that side of things.

I had developed a good friendship with Gerry Nolan, who was manager of the Frenchpark club Western Gaels and he rang me out of the blue one day to ask if I'd be interested in coming on board as a coach.

It probably came as a surprise to a lot of people, or maybe it was even seen as a step back after winning county titles as a manager, but I was looking forward to taking a back seat for a while and honing my coaching skills at a good club. It felt like a positive move and a weight lifted off my shoulders.

I would chat to Gerry and his backroom including Pat O'Gara and Enda Tully regularly, and we'd put together two or three sessions a week. It was the best of both worlds… I had control over the sessions and there was no pressure on me to chase up players or deal with any other issues that arise from time to time.

I learned a lot in Frenchpark. It was probably a step I had skipped when taking over at St Brigid's. It also opened my eyes to the realities faced by clubs in other parts of the county. In Kiltoom, we had three full-sized pitches, a small-sided pitch, and a couple of dressing-rooms. If we wanted to put on an evening session or a game in midweek that was no problem.

Western Gaels had to travel to a club which had floodlights or sometimes even as far as the Connacht Centre of Excellence in Bekan. It was like night and day – pardon the pun.

It showed me that we had been a bit spoilt at Brigid's. It really opened my eyes to how most other clubs operated.

I AM ST BRIGID'S through and through so to leave the club and then take up a position at one of our former rivals wasn't something I took lightly. The fact that we would be playing Brigid's also crossed my mind and I knew that was going to be strange. Knowing my luck, we were always going to draw them in the championship too.

I put it all out of my head and accepted Gerry's offer because, more than anything, I wanted to stay involved in the game and I knew that it would be a great experience.

I had done my homework too before arriving in Frenchpark and after chatting to some of the players I knew I was walking into a proper set-up. I also wanted to make sure that I'd be welcome as a coach after going to war against a few of those lads over the years. There was no point in me driving out there two or three times a week if lads weren't going to be listening to me.

My message to them was simple… 'If you guys are up for it ,then I am too!' I also assured them that I would give them everything I possibly could during my time there – from the first minute I walked in, there was a good buzz about the place.

THE GAELS WERE no fools either. We had a core of really good players who were playing for Roscommon at the time or who had represented the county at various levels in the past. Great fellas like Kevin Higgins, Ciaran Cafferkey, the Creggs… Seanie 'Yak' McDermott and Derek Moran. Solid lads on and off the football pitch. They were my kind of players and we got on well from the start.

If I was to be critical, they were probably just lacking two or three more really good players to be considered genuine championship contenders that year. The panel was tight enough and there were a couple of younger lads who, at that stage, were still a little bit raw. The hope was that they could make progress over the following couple of years because fresh blood coming through prevents lads from becoming too comfortable.

They probably had players in a few positions whose place in the team wasn't being put under enough pressure. They knew their jersey was safe and that can lead to complacency. It was different back in Kiltoom, where there was always a constant flow of players coming through and you knew if you didn't put maximum effort in at training or didn't perform when it mattered, then someone else would be ready to take your place.

As an older player at St Brigid's, you knew that once you lost your place it was going to be very difficult to win it back. The threat of being dropped acted as further motivation and ensured that performance levels rarely dipped throughout the year. The Gaels had a bit to go to get to that level.

They had some terrific players though. I had always found their Roscommon veteran Seanie McDermott to be a very sticky marker. He'd do anything to win and he'd be constantly in your ear driving you mad. It was a pleasure to get the opportunity to coach him at his club, where he was such an important player. He wasn't just a great footballer, he's also a genuinely lovely lad and a real winner too.

Seanie would demand high standards from all those around him during those training sessions. He drove his teammates on in matches too but unfortunately not everyone seemed willing or able to push themselves like he could.

I could see very early on why they had struggled to win a championship. There was no doubt the talent was there but there just weren't enough leaders like Seanie in the team. You have to be driven and have real belief that you can win. Western Gaels seemed to be lacking a bit in that department.

THAT'S MAYBE WHERE the difference is between the likes of St Brigid's and Clann na nGael and some of the other teams around the county. From quite a young age, players at the big two in south Roscommon are used to winning and the competition between them pushes them on.

That rivalry is something that is very evident any time you walk into the clubhouse. Any success the neighbours have can be difficult to take, even if it's in the underage competitions. It also acts as a yardstick for your own club's development.

When Clann are winning minor titles it's something that's discussed in Kiltoom, and vice versa when St Brigid's are winning. It acts as motivation for players and coaches.

There is a lot of promise in teams like Western Gaels and Boyle in terms of breaking the southern stranglehold but there are factors at play that give the clubs from Kiltoom, Johnstown and even Woodmount a big advantage.

Population, economy, and resources play a big part in how successful teams are and having a large number of players at underage levels means more of a pick when it comes to minor and senior levels.

Brigid's, Clann and Pearses are helped by the fact that they're situated close to towns like Athlone and Ballinasloe, where there are more education and employment opportunities. Being close to the M6 is also a big factor because it means lads can be in Galway or Dublin in less than an hour and a half. It's more difficult for lads travelling to Boyle or west Roscommon while working or studying in Dublin.

The quality of the facilities cannot be overlooked either. There's big money in clubs like Brigid's and Clann. It helps those clubs not only to attract young players but also to offer them good coaching from the age of six right up to senior level. Other clubs can only look on with envy at times.

Money and facilities are no substitute for hard work and commitment though and there was certainly a lot of that at Western Gaels. The talent clubs like the Gaels and Boyle have produced in recent years means they must be doing something right.

I REMEMBER BEING in the dressing-room before the championship draw in 2019 and telling Seanie that we'd get Brigid's in the championship. 'There's nothing surer, Yak,' I told him, and it was no surprise when their name came out.

I had spoken about the possibility of meeting my former club with Gerry before even accepting the role and he asked me to think about how it would feel.

I did go away at that time and think about if for a few weeks but in the meantime, I was getting phone calls from players like Seanie, Cathal Cregg and Derek Moran asking whether I was taking the job. They said it was time to refresh the training sessions and their feedback helped me to make up my mind.

Gerry also put my mind at ease by assuring me that I'd be fully focused on the training. It gave me more time to get the most out of the sessions and provide individual feedback to players too. I could focus in on the small but important details rather than worrying about the bigger picture. It was ideal.

When managing a senior team, it's almost impossible to focus on every little detail at training and that's why a good right-hand man is so important.

Unfortunately, the best coaches are usually snapped up by county teams and they can be hard to come by at club level. Top-class volunteers really are worth their weight in gold.

LOOKING BACK, I really enjoyed my time with Gerry and the Gaels. One of the highlights for me was the night we beat St Brigid's in the league. Some of the football we played that night was every bit as good as the stuff we used to play in Kiltoom.

There's nothing better than watching players moving the ball at pace, and constantly running and looking for the ball. That level of movement is nearly impossible to defend against and it's something that we tried to instil in the Gaels.

The one nagging worry that night was the fact that we should have won that game by 10 points or more. Old habits die hard for players though and our lack of ruthlessness would come back and hurt us later in the year. We still got the win that night, but we allowed Brigid's to put a gloss on the scoreboard they didn't deserve.

We came face-to-face with them again in the championship just a couple of months later. It wasn't the strongest St Brigid's side I had ever seen. But they still had quality players in every line, and had Senan Kilbride to come off the bench and kick a booming point from out near the sideline. Typical!

I had nailed my colours firmly to the Western Gaels' mast in the build-up to the game. We were training out in Doon in County Offaly – home of the great Vinny Claffey – and I was up for it. I felt I had to show the lads how much I wanted to win it just in case there were any lingering doubts about where my loyalties lay. No matter who I come up against, I want to win.

Western Gaels were all that mattered to me at that moment.

We had a brilliant week in training as we prepared for the game, and we were confident going into it. Our confidence only rose when we saw the St Brigid's starting 15 that day. While it was still a strong side, it lacked the fear factor of St Brigid's teams in the past. I felt we had a real chance.

The reception I received was fine.

You're always going to get a bit of stick when you return to a former club and it felt a little strange to be walking in with a Western Gaels top on me for a Brigid's match. But I was there to do a job for them, and nobody would have been happier with a Gaels' win that day.

Players and coaches tend to move around quite a bit in Roscommon football, but it would have been a much different story if I was coaching Clann or Pearses – like Shane Curran had done a couple of years previously. Cake was a bit of a footballing nomad anyway, having come from Castlerea in the first place.

My move to Frenchpark was made a little bit easier because as a coach I wasn't really in the spotlight. I have yet to manage a club against St Brigid's, but I think I would find that a bit strange. The club was such a big part of my life for so many years and my love for it will always be there.

AS IT TURNED out, St Brigid's' experience of the big games stood to them that day against Western Gaels. It just felt like the pressure of the championship took its toll on us and we crumbled. We looked edgy in possession and the passing was sloppy. We kept coughing up possession at crucial moments and you can't get away with that at that level.

Brigid's ran out deserving winners, but I was incredibly disappointed for Gerry and the lads afterwards. They had shown great commitment throughout the year and particularly in the weeks leading up to that game. It was tough on them.

Gerry took it the hardest and he announced he was stepping down as manager in the dressing-room immediately after the match. He said he had taken the team as far as he could and that it was now time for a fresh start.

Our performance could have been better, but we just hadn't got the rub of the green against St Brigid's either and you need luck in games of that magnitude. We were never going to close the gap on the big south Roscommon clubs in just 12 months, so I had hoped we would get another crack at it the following year.

I certainly would have stuck around if Gerry had asked me to, but then again, I hadn't been putting in the hours for as long as Gerry had and so I completely understood and respected his decision.

In the aftermath of our exit from the championship and Gerry's departure from the hot seat, he suggested that I should throw my name into the hat for the manager's job. I was flattered but I told him there was no way I could follow him. He had been there for about five years and had always put the club first.

The Gaels had won a couple of league titles in that time and I was really hoping I could help them take the next step in the championship, but it wasn't to be.

Looking back at our time together, I do think we helped bring them on another level. There were times when their movement of the football was a joy to watch, and nobody could ever fault the players' commitment levels. From forwards to backs, their intensity and work rate was very impressive.

We created plenty of chances through our quick inter-play too, I just felt we weren't quite clinical enough in front of goal at times. We'd create seven or eight goal chances some days but only come away with one or two.

You need that killer instinct and it's not something you can just turn on and off like a tap. The very best teams have it ingrained in them and when they have their foot on their opponent's throat, they squeeze. That's the level the likes of Western Gaels should be aiming for.

For me personally, it's just a pity we couldn't bring them on that little bit further. There's no doubt that is a fantastic club with some great people involved and I thoroughly enjoyed my time with them.

I WASN'T OUT of the game for long and made a return to management with Rosemount in Westmeath for the 2020 season. Unfortunately, Covid-19 arrived in March of that year and our whole season was turned upside down.

It was always going to take time to develop a good team but there were plenty of positive signs during training sessions and we performed really well against The Downs in the championship. That was a good display and gave us great confidence that we could go on and do some damage in the later rounds.

We came up against Athlone in the quarter-finals, who were led by my former coach Liam McHale. I don't think we did ourselves justice in that game and were beaten by four points in the end. It was good to see Liam again though and we promised to meet up for a few pints in Ballina whenever things got back to normal.

My time at Rosemount came to an end because I had plans to travel to China of all places as part of a business venture with a good friend of mine Fergal Kelly.

We had come up with a design for a rebounder which could be used by several teammates at the same time. The idea was to head over and meet with the company that would be producing it for us.

The chairman at Rosemount felt that with Covid and my travel plans, it was probably best to bring someone else in to continue the progress the lads had made that year. That was fair enough and there were no hard feelings on my part. I enjoyed my time there and it's a club with a lot of promise.

Our Pro Sport Rebounder will be on the market in the summer of 2021, we hope.

A hexagonal shape, it is a six-sided rebounder, with each of the sides tilting back and forward. Six players or less can use it at any one time, and there are sensors on it for target practice.

It's also good for motor skills and motor development – allowing players to develop important skills such as kicking with both the left and right foot. Same for hand-passing. It's actually brilliant for hand-eye co-ordination, and first-touch in Gaelic football, hurling and soccer.

It's one of a kind, the first of its kind ever made! We also have a one-sided rebounder in development. Both will be available to buy worldwide. It can be used by kids or professional sportspeople, and we have received a great deal of interest from professional soccer coaches in the UK, the US and Asia.

A GLOBAL PANDEMIC may have locked the whole country down at the start of 2021, but it was never going to keep me away from the sport I love! If anything, the lockdowns have just highlighted the importance of sport in our lives.

It has always been my way to escape and so I've been a bit lost without it. I think most people would agree that taking part in any sport is great for the body… and mind.

Gaelic football was always more than just an addiction to me, it was crucial in terms of my physical and mental health. It has also provided me with both real life heroes and life-long friends, and it's something that I hope remains part of my life long into the future.

EPILOGUE

PREVIOUS PAGE:

Caroline, and our boys Ryen and Jack, are my life. But, as I've said, I've been lucky to have made such outstanding friends throughout my life due to my days with St Brigid's and Roscommon. Here I am (top) with Caroline, our boys and my great friend Kieran Keaveney on a day out in Croke Park. With my mother and No. 1 fan, Rosaleen; and (bottom right) three of the best at our wedding day (my cousin Gary Dolan; my Best Man James Comiskey and the late Conor Connelly (RIP).

Epilogue

I'VE PLAYED WITH lads, who after retiring from football, would be seen cycling and running the roads. Some of them are even decked out, head to toe, in Lycra as they huff and puff their way up small hills.

I'd see them and think... *What the f**k is wrong with ye?*

It was only when I retired myself in 2016 that I finally got it. You have to be doing something and I suppose running and cycling is as good as anything else.

Me? I try to go fishing and shooting and play a bit of golf, but I could never manage to step away from football completely.

That's probably why, at the age of 42, I decided to go back playing Junior B with St Brigid's. The arrival of lockdown made me realise how much I'd miss playing if I was suddenly told I could never do it again.

I needed to stay active anyway. I would put on weight easy enough, but it was more my mental health I was worried about. I need to be letting off steam... or the head would be completely fried!

As well as playing the bit of football, I still do a bit of running in Mote Park and head to the gym when it's open. Swimming with the kids at the Abbey Hotel is also a great way of getting a bit of exercise in.

It's something I enjoy, and it keeps the body and mind half-right. If I'm active then I sleep like a baby.

It's when I stop that I run into trouble.

SIGNING UP TO play Junior B was a bit of an accident. Some of the boys had put a WhatsApp group together and added a few of the old heads. It was just after the senior team had beaten Pádraig Pearses in the 2020 county final so there were good vibes around the club at the time.

I went up to Daly's Tavern on the Monday after the final to meet a few of them for a pint and they were at me to join up.

'Ah stop lads… I'm 42 years of age and the body is fecked!'

I had recently had an operation on my nose and if I took a whack on it, it would mean more surgery, more health expenses. More time off work.

These are things that matter in your forties.

I didn't commit to coming back that night, but I stayed lurking in the WhatsApp group out of curiosity. Suddenly, there were more and more thumbs up for the games and I found it harder to resist. There was no training – turn up for the game, and head for pints after. It sounded good to me!

Like any recovering addict, I started justifying my decision to go back to Caroline and anyone else who'd listen.

'Sure, it's a bit of craic… it'll be good for me!'

'There won't be any training… so I can just show up for the games.'

That kind of thing.

Of course, most of the lads with their thumbs up never bothered their backsides showing up for the games. So, there I was, togging out next to young lads at the ripe old age of 42.

We went out to play St Dominic's one of the nights in what I thought was a league match but was actually the championship. It didn't matter what competition it was to me though, because I was still getting stuck in. I don't know whether that's a good thing or a bad thing anymore.

I picked up an injury another night playing against Roscommon Gaels. I was one-on-one with their goalkeeper Mick Byrne and smashed the ball through his legs. Poor Mick then fell on his backside as he ran back to his goal to fish the ball out of his net.

I started laughing at him as I slowed down to a jog.

I wasn't laughing for long. As I came to a stop, I felt the hamstring go and it was soon Mick's turn to laugh at me as I was helped off the pitch. Karma I suppose!

IT'S A PITY it had to finish up early due to lockdown because I enjoyed being back out there. It was great craic but a poor substitute for the do-or-die feeling of a big championship match in front of thousands of people.

Having said that, it was probably the biggest crowd they've had down for a Junior B match in a few years. Word must have leaked that a few of old veterans were making a comeback and people couldn't resist coming down to have a laugh at us. I was just glad the jersey still fit even though it was a bit tighter than I remembered!

THE START DATE of the 2021 GAA season hadn't even been confirmed when I agreed to take over Offaly junior side Doon. I just can't seem to be able to stay away from football, so I suppose I'm lucky that Caroline is so understanding.

But where does it end?

I hope not for a long time anyway. It's all part of this journey I'm on to become a better coach and manager. The different perspective I'll gain at Doon will only help me in the long run.

My ultimate goal? It has to be to manage my county at senior level. Or else, what's the point? I have a few regrets in life, and the way things were left during my playing days with Roscommon is definitely something which still bothers me.

I wish I had come out and explained the situation around my departure from Tommy Carr's panel in 2005 and told the supporters why I decided to walk away. It had nothing to do with falling out of love with Roscommon. I had just grown disillusioned with my role in the team.

I should also have declined John Maughan's offer of a return in 2008. My heart wasn't in it by that stage and I don't think it was ever really going to work out after we got off on the wrong foot at the start of his reign. It was a real pity too because I was probably in some of the best form of my career at that time.

BEING INVOLVED IN the game is something that will always be important to me. I have loved covering games for different media outlets, whether it was Shannonside FM with Willie Hegarty, Ocean FM with John Lynch or RTÉ Radio with Brian Carthy.

It is a great way to see games that otherwise I might never get to attend and watch. There is a great buzz to commentating on a live game, giving my opinion... trying to capture the imagination of those listening... whether they are in Roscommon, Donegal, Dublin or Kerry... the UK, the States, Dubai or Australia.

WHETHER I WAS involved or not though, I always wanted Roscommon to win, and still do. There were some elements of the set-up I didn't agree with during my playing days and certain members of the county board and some management teams that I struggled to see eye-to-eye with. But none of that mattered whenever the ball was thrown in.

Who knows, maybe one day I will be given one more opportunity to bring success to the county I love.

Then the slate could really be wiped clean.